a better YOU experience

CANDACE WILLIAMS

LifeRich PUBLISHING®

LifeRich Publishing is a registered trademark of
The Reader's Digest Association, Inc.

LifeRich Publishing books may be ordered through booksellers or by contacting:

LifeRich Publishing
1663 Liberty Drive
Bloomington, IN 47403
www.liferichpublishing.com
844-686-9607

ISBN: 978-1-4897-4787-7 (sc)
ISBN: 978-1-4897-4789-1 (hc)
ISBN: 978-1-4897-4788-4 (e)

Library of Congress Control Number: 2023914757

Print information available on the last page.

LifeRich Publishing rev. date: 09/27/2023

Contents

Foreword

As a school psychologist for nearly fifteen years, I've seen first-hand the impact of how decisions made in one's young adult years can influence outcomes and realities later in life.

Since we met in kindergarten, Candace and I didn't know that our lives would parallel and that we would actually walk an integral part of our journeys together. After losing contact in junior high school, we discovered that we were sitting in a worship service one Sunday morning, and we've been inseparable ever since.

Before that unexpected meeting, we were unaware that we had both been in emotionally bankrupt romantic relationships with men we loved and adored, but the relationships were leading nowhere! We wore our external smiles and would meet up for our BFF bonding moments over fine dining and weekend brunches. However, we were both aching inside. This was partly because we longed for a lover who would treat us right and be the men we ultimately needed them to be! Besides, we were both great catches! Candace had a booming career, she drove a luxury car, she had a beautiful city apartment, and she was simply waiting for love to find her.

I had obtained my third degree in psychology, also drove a luxury vehicle, had excellent credit, and was wondering why the man I loved hadn't chosen me as his wife. What Candace and I needed most was a lover of our souls, and we would never thirst again (John 4:13–14 NIV).

After receiving a promotion in my field, I changed employers and moved to suburbia. It was in this move that I felt incredibly alone but closer to God than ever before. Ironic, right?

I noticed a change in myself: I simply wanted more of God! Finding a man became less important, and wanting to please God became paramount. Similarly, I noticed a change in Candace. She started talking less and less about men and more about wanting to invest in quality friendships and meaningful bonds. At that point, unbeknown to us, we became accountability partners. We spent countless moments conversing about God's desires for our lives.

> Sweet friendships refresh the soul and awaken our
> hearts with joy, for good friends are like the anointing
> oil that yields the fragrant incense of God's presence.
> (Proverbs 27:9 TPT)

Having walked parallel paths filled with triumphs and failures, poor decisions and excellent ones, there is a validity that comes from the authenticity of one's lived experience. Candace gives a bird's-eye view of how her failed attempts at living a life without God led to her truly living her best life with God at the center of it all! She details topics that range from struggles in romantic relationships to internal battles with self to familial dynamics that leave readers in awe of her resiliency. The authenticity of this book will take you on a journey that will have you captivated and intrigued about how to start your journey to becoming a better you!

As a woman who has walked a journey of self-discovery and learned by experience alone, having this book in my repertoire would have alleviated tearful nights, moments of regret, and questions of whether I made the right decision. This book will provide you with the tools necessary to evolve into a better version of yourself with the confidence that you are on the right road! This book is synonymous with having a life coach at your fingertips in book form!

The practical applications and tools offered here can be applied to your life now and in the future.

Tamika Sanders, EdS, NCSP

Preface

Better /bedar/: **of a more excellent or effective type or quality.**
[Oxford Dictionary]

I made the decision to work on self-improvement because I realized that attracting better things in life starts with me. As I strive to become a better version of myself, I know that I will naturally attract better opportunities and experiences. The key lies in personal growth and self-development, and I am determined to embrace this journey wholeheartedly. The more I invest in my own growth, the more positivity and abundance I will attract into my life!

Hello, everyone! I'm Candace. I'm excited to share the story behind A Better You Experience, which was inspired by a transformative moment in my life. It happened on a particularly gloomy afternoon when I parked my car at work, feeling overwhelmed and burdened by the careless decisions I had made throughout my young adult years. The downward spiral of my life and the emotional roller coaster had taken their toll.

In that moment, I had a profound realization that I needed a change. I was determined not to continue living without God's guidance. With sincerity in my heart, I offered a short yet sincere prayer, and that marked the turning point in my life. From that moment onward, everything began to shift for the better:

Heavenly Father, I come before you with a humble heart. I desire your presence and guidance in my life. I acknowledge that my way has not always been aligned with your will, and I now surrender my desires to yours. I earnestly seek to walk closely with you, and I yearn for your divine plan to unfold in my life. Please, dear God, enter my heart and cleanse me from my sins and the mistakes I've made. Grant me the strength to learn from my past and move forward with wisdom and grace. I long to live a purposeful and fulfilled life, one that is devoted to serving you and others. Thank you for your unending love and forgiveness. I commit to following your lead and seeking your guidance in every aspect of my life. May I be a vessel of your light and love, shining brightly in the world around me. With faith and trust in your providence, I pray this with all my heart. Amen.

I wrote A Better You Experience to inspire young women to reach for their highest potential and discover their true selves through a connection with God. This book serves as a guiding light, leading readers towards aligning with God's will and purpose for their lives. Within its pages, you'll gain valuable insights into my personal journey—how God molded my mindset and enabled me to evolve into a stronger, more fulfilled woman. I firmly believe that, with unwavering faith and determination, we can overcome any obstacles and embrace lives of fulfilment and purpose. Remember, this journey is not a sprint; it's a marathon. Every day presents an opportunity to become better than we were before. Let's embark on this transformative journey together and strive to become the best versions of ourselves. I made a conscious decision to strive for improvement, recognizing that it all begins with personal growth. As I progress and evolve, with God, I am confident that the positive changes within myself will naturally attract better opportunities and experiences.

My hope in sharing my experiences is twofold: firstly, to offer women the opportunity to learn from my mistakes, and secondly, to inspire them to embark on their own path of personal growth, pursuing the fulfilment and purpose that await them.

This book is for you if:

+ You find yourself exhausted from repeating the same mistakes.
+ You are grappling with issues related to self-esteem.
+ You desire positive change in your life but lack the appropriate tools to grow into a better version of yourself.
+ You yearn for more fulfilment and purpose in your life.
+ You seek to identify and strengthen your connection with your faith, specifically with Christ.
+ You aim to cultivate a deeper and more meaningful relationship with Christ.
+ You are eager to uncover the hidden, better side of your true self.

Acknowledgments

When you're on a journey to becoming a better person, there are moments when you'll find yourself seeking comfort in discomfort. During those tender moments, I felt lonely and struggled through numerous sleepless nights, unable to see the light at the end of the tunnel. However, I persisted in choosing God and His path, which eventually led to personal growth and a better version of myself, even though it didn't feel that way at first.

In my quest to become a better version of myself, I fervently prayed for divine guidance, pleading, "God, please send me my team." Gratitude fills my heart as God graciously granted my request, connecting me with like-minded individuals who not only uplift and encourage me but also hold me accountable on this transformative journey. Among these cherished souls is my dear sister, Titania, whose unwavering love and the unbreakable bond we've nurtured over the past nine years have profoundly shaped the woman I am today.

To my sister-cousin, Michele, I extend my deepest thanks for your unwavering affection. Your presence in my life during the times of greatest need has been a profound source of comfort. I still remember the moment I surrendered my heart and life to God, with you on the other end of the line, a compassionate listener to my tears.

That act of kindness shall forever be etched in my heart, and I will always cherish our connection.

For my beloved cousins, Jessica and Lucinda, you have been my pillars of accountability, my ever-ready companions in those moments when I needed a gentle nudge to keep moving forward. Your impactful conversations and unyielding motivation have been invaluable, propelling me through life's challenges with renewed determination.

To my sister, confidante, and dearest friend, Tamika, words cannot express the depth of my gratitude. Your unwavering patience and constant support have meant the world to me on this daunting journey called life. Your presence has been a soothing balm, and I treasure every moment we share.

My heartfelt appreciation goes out to my brother, Grady. Your honesty and steadfast reminders of my true identity have been a beacon of clarity in times of doubt. Your unwavering belief in me has been a source of strength, and I am forever indebted to your unwavering presence in my life.

I am grateful for the unwavering love and support of my cherished family and exceptional support system. Your unconditional care and dedication have touched my heart in ways words can scarcely express. To Annie Verdie, Dawn Marie, Jadea Marie, and Aunty Lucinda, thank you for being the backbone of my journey, for standing by my side through both triumphs and trials. Your presence on my team fills me with strength, comfort, and inspiration.

Dearest Daddy, I am filled with gratitude for your unwavering presence in my life, especially during the times when it truly counted. Your constant belief in me and the way you wholeheartedly recognize my potential have left an indelible mark on my soul. Your encouraging words, assuring me that everything I undertake is remarkable, resonate deeply within me and will remain etched in my heart for all time. Mommy, your boundless tenderness, love, patience, and kindness have bestowed upon me immeasurable blessings. Words cannot adequately express the depth of affection I hold for you. I am humbled and privileged to be in a position where I can reciprocate the care and support you have selflessly showered upon me. Together, you both have played pivotal roles in shaping the person I have become. Your unconditional love and unwavering support have been the foundation upon which I have built my life. With hearts overflowing with appreciation, I cherish the love and guidance you have bestowed upon me, and I eagerly look forward to creating many more treasured moments together.

PK—Queen Prophetess Katara—you are the crowning glory of this journey. With divine inspiration, you have propelled everyone to reach greater heights. Our faithful prophetic gatherings every Friday night over the past three years have been instrumental in propelling me toward my destiny. Your impact on my life is immeasurable, and I am eternally blessed to be connected with you.

Together, we form an unbreakable bond that enriches my life beyond measure. With utmost gratitude, I extend my heartfelt appreciation for each of you, for you are the pillars that make my world brighter and my heart lighter.

Introduction

Bumpy Beginnings

The ultimate aspiration is to cultivate an extraordinary and profound relationship with Christ, embracing the boundless blessings within His kingdom. As appealing as this goal may be, achieving it proves to be a journey of its own complexities. Personally, I have discovered that the path towards such a connection with Christ is far from effortless; it demands dedication, self-reflection, and spiritual growth. Nonetheless, the pursuit of this divine bond is undeniably rewarding, unlocking a world of abundant grace and fulfilment.

From an external perspective, I can genuinely say that I had a wonderful childhood. Growing up in a middle-class family, I was fortunate to have both my parents living under the same roof. My father, in particular, went above and beyond for our family. He tirelessly worked one full-time job and even during the holidays each year, he would take up a part-time job just to ensure we woke up to smiles on Christmas morning, greeted by a towering stack of gifts.

Over the passing years, my mother's mental well-being gradually deteriorated as she faced the burdens and challenges that life presents. I distinctly recall the poignant moments when, after school, I would visit her at a mental institution. The heartbreaking reality of being separated by a glass barrier prevented any physical connection; I longed to hold her, offer comfort, and express my love. Even now, discussing these memories, my emotions remain raw, and tears well up in my eyes. I sincerely pray for grace and healing for my beloved mother.

Though she continues to grapple with her own battles, she has evolved since those difficult days when I was just a thirteen-year-old, observing her through the restrictive lens of a glass partition, almost a quarter-century ago. Despite the hurdles she faces, she has grown, and the woman before me now is not the same mother I knew back then.

During that time, it goes without saying that I faced significant struggles as a teenager. Adapting to various challenges while managing my pain and keeping up with school became an immense burden. My high school years were marked by constant fights and conflicts. One incident stands out when I lost my temper and impulsively punched a guy in the face. The trigger was him slamming the door just as I was approaching, resulting in my tardiness for class. This rash act led to my arrest, with my hands restrained behind my back, and a visit to the police station awaited my parents. Upon seeing the tall, imposing boy I had fought, my mom asked, "Candace, is this who you fought?" I replied defiantly, "Yes, and anyone can get these hands if they want them." Looking back, I acknowledge how awful my behavior was during those times.

Embarking on my academic journey, I set out to pursue higher education at college. Unfortunately, an unfortunate incident led to my expulsion and suspension due to an unintended but significant disruption caused on that particular day. As I sat in the passenger seat of my father's Mercedes-Benz on the way back home, surrounded by ten bags of personal belongings in the back seat and trunk, I maintained an outwardly composed demeanor, though a faint smile betrayed my true feelings. My father's expression on the other hand, displayed unmistakable dissatisfaction, leaving no doubt that, given different circumstances, he might have chosen to leave me stranded on the roadside, though he would never truly abandon me. My dad has always been an unwavering supporter, standing up for me regardless of any negative perceptions about my actions. Despite his disappointment, he continues to believe in my potential.

In my defense, I found myself in a situation where my friend was being subjected to bullying, and we were confronted with physical aggression initially. Let me be clear: I am not one to engage in bullying or provoke conflicts; instead, I firmly believe in standing up for myself and others when necessary. Nevertheless, I acknowledge that this does not excuse any form of irresponsibility on my part. It is essential to recognize that many of our unfortunate choices are often influenced by our circumstances and realities. However, the crucial question we must address is how long we are willing to perpetuate these recurring mistakes. I must admit, at the time, I found myself lacking an immediate answer to that question.

As I looked up, I was startled to realize that a whole decade had passed, and it struck me that I had allowed myself to go through an emotional roller coaster with a man who wasn't my husband. Then, there was another year spent with someone who felt like a heaven-sent blessing—not because he was my husband, but because that relationship played a pivotal role in shaping the woman I am today. My enduring belief is that he was undoubtedly heaven-sent, for his actions consistently challenged and pushed me to my limits, sometimes even driving me up the wall. It was when I found myself at my wit's end that I realized the invaluable lesson he taught me.

If I had not experienced such moments of intense frustration, I am confident that I would have remained stuck, making the same countless mistakes repeatedly without ever learning from them.

It was a gloomy morning as I sat in the parking lot of my job, overwhelmed with the weight of my sins. In that moment, I reached out to God, inviting Him into my heart and pleading for forgiveness. Tears streamed down my cheeks, and I felt a deep desire for change. Trying to transform my life on my own had proven futile, and I knew it was time to surrender to God's ways.

I decided to give God's path a chance, acknowledging that my way had led to disappointment. Soon after making this decision, my life underwent a profound transformation, and it only took thirty days for the change to become evident. All God asks for is our wholehearted devotion and unwavering focus. In return, He offers us boundless possibilities and blessings beyond measure. The power to choose lies with us.

Indeed, my life significantly improved, thanks to God's favor and grace that showered upon me throughout that year. I am eternally grateful for His divine presence and the positive impact it has had on my life.

It was a gloomy morning when I found myself sitting in the parking lot of my job, overwhelmed with a deep desire for change. In that moment, I turned to God and asked Him to come into my heart, seeking His forgiveness for my sins. Tears welled up in my eyes as I acknowledged that I could no longer continue down the same path. Despite my previous attempts to change on my own, I had come to realize that my efforts had been in vain.

I reached a pivotal point in my life, where I felt compelled to embrace God's ways and surrender to His guidance. I thought to myself, "My way hasn't worked, so perhaps I should try it God's way." Little did I know that this decision would transform my life profoundly.

Remarkably, within a mere thirty days, I noticed the positive impact of my newfound connection with God. All He desired was our wholehearted devotion and undivided attention, and in return, He promised to bestow His blessings upon us, granting us the world. As I reflect on that period, I cannot help but marvel at the remarkable changes that unfolded.

Truly, my life took a turn for the better, and I am immensely grateful for God's favor and the blessings He showered upon me throughout that year. His intervention and presence in my life have made all the difference, illuminating my path and guiding me toward a more fulfilling and purposeful existence.

I received a surprising phone call from my boss, asking if I would be interested in a potential opportunity in Baton Rouge, Louisiana. At that time, I was living in Chicago, and the sudden offer caught me off guard. I couldn't help but wonder, "Where the heck did this come from?"

In that moment, I turned to my faith and sought guidance from God. I asked, "How do you feel about that?" Deep in my heart, I felt a sense of conviction that this opportunity was the right path for me to take. I must admit; it became evident to me that it was both God's will and the right decision to pursue. I truly believe that if it aligned with God's plan, then it was undeniably the right thing to do.

I was living with my aunt at the time, confined to a small space in her home and sleeping on a sofa chair in her bedroom. However, my life took a significant turn, and I finally got a place of my own in Baton Rouge. The way we live our lives reflects who we truly are. God's plans for us are never mediocre; He wants us to live according to His will so that He can bless us with the very best. And so it happened – I was promoted to my second assignment, earning more than six figures, and no longer living with my aunt.

To clarify, giving ourselves to God is not about expecting something in return. It's essential to avoid entering a relationship with God with selfish motives, solely focusing on personal benefits. Rather, the act of giving ourselves to God should be selfless and done without any anticipation of receiving something in return. As Psalm 37:4 NIV suggests, we are encouraged to delight in the Lord, and in doing so, He will fulfill the desires of our hearts. It is God who plants these desires within us and subsequently grants them to us. This showcases God's goodness and His role in guiding our paths.

Since I am no longer living in sin and have discerned that God has placed something in my heart to pursue, I have decided to follow His will and have relocated to Baton Rouge.

My experience there was undeniably tough and lonely. Without any family or friends by my side, I felt completely isolated. Nevertheless, I knew I had to persevere and avoid falling back into my old, unhealthy habits. Surrendering my life to God wasn't an easy task; it demanded sincere effort and hard work, akin to cultivating any other meaningful relationship.

Prior to moving to Louisiana, I had always sought companionship in a partner and never embraced being single for long. The fear of being alone led me to rely on alcohol as a means to numb the pain, eventually leading me down the path of alcoholism. Each morning, I found myself reaching for a bottle of wine, and another awaited me every evening.

When the opportunity to move to Baton Rouge presented itself, I viewed it as God's way of granting me a fresh start. I saw this as an opportunity to prove my responsibility to Him. Without hesitation, I decided to break away from alcohol, vowing not to touch wine or champagne again.

Throughout this journey, I learned the importance of starving distractions and prioritizing my focus to reach the path and purpose that God has in store for my life. It's an ongoing process, but I'm determined to stay committed to my faith and personal growth.

Prior to relocating to Louisiana, I had always sought companionship in a partner and rarely embraced being single for an extended period. Unfortunately, the fear of being alone led me to rely on alcohol as a way to numb the pain, which eventually spiralled into alcoholism. Every morning, I found myself reaching for a bottle of wine, and another one waited for me every evening. However, when the opportunity to move to Baton Rouge presented itself, I viewed it as a chance for a fresh start, a divine intervention in my life. To me, it felt like God was granting me an opportunity to prove my responsibility to Him. Without any hesitation, I made the resolute decision to break away from alcohol, vowing as a part of my healing journey, to refrain from drinking wine or champagne.

Throughout this transformative journey, I came to understand the significance of starving distractions and focusing on my priorities to align with the path and purpose that God has in store for my life. Although it remains an ongoing process, I am resolute in staying committed to my faith and personal growth.

Despite tremendous struggles in finding a church home and making friends, my unwavering faith in God never faltered. He kept me safe and protected. I once received a prophecy that urged me not to grow weary in doing good, and that's precisely what I was feeling. However, my obedience to God led to a short-term blessing—an opportunity to work at one of the busiest stores in the company, located in Corpus Christi, Texas.

Being back in Corpus Christi meant relying solely on God since I had no friends there. While Texas wasn't the smoothest experience for me, it proved to be exactly what I needed for my personal growth. It was in Texas that I discovered my purpose and was pushed beyond my limits. The challenges I faced there were rough, and I often found myself ridiculed without much support. Nevertheless, I had God by my side. Countless nights were spent in tears due to the tough and demanding nature of my work. As a young woman leading one of the highest volume stores in the company, I faced not just the busyness but constant resistance and pushback. Nonetheless, I persevered, ensuring I fulfilled my duties as a leader.

At times, we fail to realize that when we walk with God, it is all about working together for our good. Even the pressures of everyday life can work together for our benefit. Spending quality time alone with God, free from distractions, creates a space where God can speak to us on a deeper level that might not be experienced amidst the background noise.

After surrendering to God, I made a series of transformative moves in my life. Departing from Chicago, I sought solace in Louisiana before an opportunity beckoned me to Texas. These relocations weren't driven by ambitions for promotions; rather, they were motivated by my desire to deepen my relationship with Christ and draw closer to God, dedicating myself solely to Him. I yearned to lean on His guidance, converse with Him openly, and develop an intimate understanding of His divine presence. Embracing obedience to His will, I have come to witness the blessings that flow from sowing the seeds of faith.

As time passed in Texas, a profound realization dawned upon me: life held a deeper significance beyond the confines of a job. It was as if a light had finally illuminated my path. Embracing solitude, I discovered myself evolving into the woman God had intended me to be. His purpose for me was to serve as an inspiring example, sharing and imparting to fellow women in the body of Christ the boundless love God bestows upon us. My mission became crystal clear—I yearned to spare young women the myriad of mistakes I once made. While Texas had been a significant chapter, I sensed it was not my final destination. A grander calling awaited me, though at that time, I could not put my finger on it.

After updating my résumé, I received a text from a friend and former colleague regarding an exciting opportunity in Atlanta. I gladly shared my résumé with him, and to my delight, after two months of rigorous interviews, I was offered the position. As with my previous career moves, I turned to prayer and sought God's guidance to ensure I was making the right decision. His validation gave me the confidence to accept the offer wholeheartedly.

Moving to Atlanta was undoubtedly a divine intervention. It was a moment when my purpose became crystal clear, and I discerned God's calling for my life. Without hesitation, I took action. My mission is to inspire, empower, and uplift women, encouraging them to strive for personal growth and betterment. I am conscious of not generalizing women's experiences, as I can only speak for myself. Regrettably, I once settled for less and had a challenging start. My own inhibitions hindered my path to success.

However, a profound realization dawned on me, unveiling the boundless potential we possess with God by our side. Embracing our identity in Him transforms our lives for the better. Witnessing the sheer brilliance of countless women around the world, I realized that we hold the key to our success. Some may have achieved financial prosperity, yet still feel a void—a missing link in their lives, and that link is God.

True transformation comes with obedience to God, reshaping our world, our perspectives, and our self-image. Each day, I strive to make decisions that align with God's purpose for my life. As I share my journey through this book, my heartfelt prayer is that it blesses you profoundly, encouraging you to reflect on your life, and allowing God's grace to flow through you, shining for His glory.

Tired of repeatedly making countless mistakes? It's essential to recognize that mistakes are not always intentional; they can happen even when you put in effort. One crucial aspect of life is ensuring that you place God at the forefront of everything you do. Reflecting on my own journey, I spent my entire teenage and early adult years making mistakes, such as getting into trouble at school and dating the wrong people. I found myself stuck in a cycle of repeating these mistakes. However, everything changed for the better when I decided to align my desires with God's plan for my life. It was a turning point. I learned that nurturing a relationship with Christ requires effort and dedication, similar to any friendship or significant other. It doesn't come easily, but dedicating genuine and meaningful time to Christ is vital. Embrace this path, and you'll witness positive transformations in your life.

That moment you realize you're fighting every day, and it's no longer comfortable. God made it that way. If he allowed you to get comfortable, you would never be able to see your destiny.

Father God, in the name of Jesus, I want you; I need you. I no longer want to do things my way and on my own. I want to walk with you, and I want only what you want for me and my life. Please, God, come into my heart. Forgive me for my sins and poor decisions. I want to live with purpose and a fulfilled life with you.

Amen.

/

HOW TO SUSTAIN DURING CELIBACY

Waiting for marriage, my journey, my path, my calling.

How can a young person stay on the path of purity?
By living according to your word.

—Psalm 119:9 NIV

A voluntary vow of sexual abstinence is the choice I've made for myself, deciding to refrain from any sexual acts until marriage. To stay true to this commitment, I have actively chosen to distance myself from anything that might lead to sex, including monitoring my thoughts, being selective about what I watch on TV, and the music I listen to. When I do date, I am careful to ensure that the process is carried out with respect and integrity. It has been over eight years since I made this decision to save myself for my future husband, and I am determined to uphold it, even if it means waiting for another ten years or more.

Let me share with you my journey over the past several years, depicting how I have grown in my relationship with Christ. One crucial aspect that I quickly realized was the necessity of wholehearted commitment. To build and sustain a genuine connection with God, I couldn't afford to be half-hearted, wavering between devotion and indifference. I had to surrender all aspects of my life to Him, without picking and choosing what to give.

To be candid, many of us, as women, tend to keep sex as a means of control and reward for when our partners behave as we desire. We might find ourselves offering our bodies as a token of appreciation. In my case, sex was the one thing I held onto tightly and refused to let go of. I used to convince myself that since I was doing everything else right, maybe continuing to be intimate with the man in my life at that time would eventually lead to marriage. In my flawed thinking, I believed that once I had achieved that, everything, including my relationship with God, would be perfect.

Oh, how mistaken I was! It didn't lead to the blissful embrace of marriage. Instead, I discovered the painful truth – he betrayed my trust and cheated on me with multiple women. He was the person who shared the prime of my twenties, and regrettably, ten precious years of my life were squandered. Despite giving my all in the beginning, his infidelity tested my resilience, and like many strong women, I initially chose to endure the heartache. Nonetheless, I ultimately mustered the strength to sever the ties that bound us. The emotional toll was overwhelming, leaving me feeling sick to my very core."

During that period, I found myself struggling without leaning on God. I neglected prayer, fasting, and seeking genuine healing, and instead, I turned to alcohol as a crutch. Regrettably, this led to the development of an alcohol addiction, with wine becoming my constant companion. I used alcohol as a means to numb the pain and escape from the harsh realities of life. What began as a simple glass of wine escalated into consuming a whole bottle after work, another when I woke up in the morning, and two bottles before bedtime. My diet consisted mainly of wine and chips, causing me to lose a significant amount of weight, dropping down to 115 pounds. This was alarming since those in my village who knew me well were aware that I had always had a more substantial physique. Losing so much weight was a major concern for everyone around me, as they questioned my well-being. Reflecting on those times now, it's truly disheartening. I was not in a good place mentally or physically.

I received some bad advice from friends and family members. Surprisingly, not a single person encouraged me to seek solace in my faith or prayed with me during difficult times. Instead, I was given harmful advice like, "You're just stressing yourself out unnecessarily. You'll face problems with the next man anyway, so you might as well settle down with this one." Additionally, they said, "If everything is peaceful at home, and he's fulfilling his responsibilities towards you and the household, why are you stirring up trouble? Don't jeopardize a good thing, Candace; you'll end up single." Lastly, I was told, "All men cheat," but I firmly believe that such a generalization is untrue.

In retrospect, I understand the importance of seeking guidance in my faith and relying on positive influences. It's essential to surround ourselves with people who support our growth and lead us towards healthier decisions.

God has someone out there just for you, someone who desires only you. I am truly grateful that I didn't heed the poor advice that was given to me. My ability to cut off ties is strong, and I must admit, I'm quite proud of it. When it comes to my peace and sanity, I refuse to compromise, even if it means taking some time to navigate through the process. Therefore, I made the resolute decision to pack up and leave the tumultuous ten-year roller-coaster ride that I once called a relationship.

I walked away from that relationship, and it was tough. Fortunately, I had my aunt to lean on during that challenging time. About a week before I decided to break up with my boyfriend, I reached out to her and asked if it would be alright to stay with her for a little while. She warmly welcomed me with open arms, and I'm incredibly grateful to God for providing me with such a supportive aunt.

While I was staying with her, I experienced some growing pains. I took the opportunity to spend time alone with both God and my thoughts. This introspective period revealed a lot about who I am and helped me understand my next steps as a single woman. It was a significant time of transition for me.

Not long after I moved in with my aunt, a significant turning point came when I received a phone call from my boss. He offered me a second executive role with a signing bonus, and without hesitation, I accepted, leading me to leave Chicago for Louisiana. From the moment I made that decision, it seemed like God started orchestrating opportunities and blessings in my life. I excelled in my new position and was eventually offered the chance to run the highest volume store in Texas. So, I moved to Texas and called it home for the next two years.

While in Texas, my focus was solely on God. During that time, I received an unexpected call to work for a different company, a change that turned out to be both personally and professionally beneficial, affirming my trust in the voice of God. I then made the next move to Georgia, where I embarked on a journey of self-discovery and self-love. Embracing the woman God created me to be, I found strength in my boldness, impactfulness, beauty, and brilliance. It became clear to me that I wanted to live my life for God and be a vessel for His love to shine through me.

My desire was for people to see God's presence in me, rather than merely material possessions like cars, homes, clothes, or wealth. I also came to the realization that I didn't want to follow the same path as some other Christian women I had encountered during my young adult years in church settings. Although they preached abstinence and saving oneself for marriage, their actions didn't always align with their words as they engaged in sexual relationships with their then-boyfriends, now husbands. I want to emphasize that my intention is not to pass judgment on them, but rather to express my genuine desire to be a living example and allow God to work through me. As part of my commitment to my faith, I made the significant decision to give up all sexual acts, embracing a celibate lifestyle. I won't deny that it's been challenging, but staying sober, remaining focused on God, and being dedicated to my goals and dreams have helped me stay on track. Through this journey, I hope to inspire others to walk their own paths of faith and to find the courage to live in alignment with their values and beliefs.

I share my story not to boast but to encourage others to trust in God's guidance and let His love lead their lives. When we surrender to His will, we discover the strength to make choices that honor Him and align with our spiritual journeys, even when the path is not easy.

In sharing my journey, I want you all to know that it is possible to walk this path of faith and self-discovery. It requires dedication, resilience, and unwavering faith in God. By staying true to ourselves and our purpose, we can find fulfilment and be a shining example for others seeking a deeper connection with God.

I had a sincere desire to invite God to dwell within me and dedicate my entire being, including my body, to Him, which led me to commit to abstaining from sex before marriage. Deciding to wait until my wedding day for intimacy was a choice I made, and I have remained steadfast in this commitment.

Reflecting on the heartache, tears, and pain I experienced in my previous relationship when I followed my own path, I eventually embraced God's guidance. Embracing His way has proven to be the best decision of my life. Living my adult years wholeheartedly devoted to God brings an incredible sense of fulfilment. Honesty and righteousness are guiding my life, and it feels incredibly rewarding to walk this path.

Choosing celibacy has allowed me to liberate myself from spiritual entanglements that I needed to break free from naturally. Engaging in sexual relationships with others can be a daunting experience, and in my case, it went beyond concerns about pregnancy or STDs; it involved a belief in the transfer of spirits. A vivid memory comes to mind when I was with my ex-partner. Despite knowing he was involved with other women sexually, I still chose to be with him. In retrospect, I noticed how I unintentionally adopted traits of the women he was seeing, and they, in turn, started behaving like me. It wasn't mere imitation driven by admiration; rather, it felt like something deeper, as if spirits were being exchanged.

It became evident as they began dressing, talking, and even walking like me. An incident stands out when a woman asked if I was trying to emulate the physique of another woman he was involved with. Although I had no conscious intention to do so, the connection through our shared partner seemed to unconsciously transform me. This unhealthy dynamic led to mental instability and made me realize that this situation was anything but beneficial for me.

Through this experience, I came to the realization that celibacy was the path to take to regain my sense of self, personal boundaries, and inner peace. By abstaining from sexual relationships, I have found the freedom to connect with my true essence and avoid the entanglements that once caused turmoil in my life. It has been a journey of self-discovery and empowerment that continues to strengthen my spiritual well-being.

We often overlook the negative impacts that engaging in sex before marriage can have on our mental well-being. First Corinthians 6:16–17 reminds us, "And don't you realize that if a man joins himself to a prostitute, he becomes one body with her? For the Scriptures say, 'The two are united into one.' But the person who is joined to the Lord is one spirit with him." This verse emphasizes the spiritual and emotional connection formed when we become intimate with someone. We merge not just physically but also mentally and emotionally.

I once experienced this first hand when I was living in sin, engaging in premarital sex. The person I was involved with was dealing with significant mental challenges, leading him to withdraw from his family and friends. Strangely, I found myself spiraling into a dark place as well. While I've always been an introvert, I withdrew even further, preferring isolation. It was as if I had become a part of him, and he, a part of me. The situation wasn't healthy at all.

Even when I was in a relationship, a time when happiness should prevail, I felt sad and miserable, mainly because he felt that way. His own unhappiness and insecurities were transferred to me, creating an unhealthy emotional entanglement. This is precisely what soul ties are all about. They lead to an exchange of energies, both positive and negative.

It's crucial to understand the impact of our actions and choices on our mental and emotional well-being. Engaging in sexual intimacy within the boundaries of marriage can promote healthier relationships, while premarital sex can result in negative consequences that affect our overall well-being and spiritual growth.

By choosing to remain sexually abstinent, I find that my mind is clear and focused. I sincerely embrace the idea of being a vessel for God's glory, allowing Him to work through me. My desire is not only to encourage and motivate others but also to lead by example. I don't claim to be perfect, but I have faced challenges in my life and made positive changes, all the while placing my trust in God throughout the process.

When your mind is clear and free, you can contemplate life without distractions. Engaging in sex can cloud your thoughts. However, since embracing celibacy, I have found the ability to genuinely listen to God's voice and make myself available for His plans in my life. Once I decided to live my life wholeheartedly, I witnessed doors opening that would have remained closed had I not surrendered myself to God. During my time with my ex, there was little room for God, as He desires our undivided attention. It was as if God was patiently waiting for me to commit wholeheartedly, so He could truly reside within me and use me for His glory.

> Do you not know that your bodies are temples of the
> Holy Spirit, who is in you, whom you have received
> from God? You are not your own; you were bought
> at a price. Therefore honor God with your bodies.
> (1 Corinthians 6:19-20 NIV)

Ladies, it is essential for us to value and cherish our bodies. Our bodies are sacred and belong to the Lord, so it is crucial not to give ourselves away to men casually. We must reserve that intimacy for our husbands alone. If you find yourself in a situation where you are involved intimately with someone who is not your spouse, remember that it's never too late to make a change. You can choose to prioritize your relationship with God and communicate this decision to your partner. A loving and respectful partner will honor your choice and wishes.

For those of you who are single and waiting for your future husband, approach dating and relationships in alignment with God's principles. Strive to follow His ways and remain true to your values.

Remember, each one of us deserves love, respect, and a relationship built on a strong foundation of faith and trust. Let us honor ourselves and our connection with God by making wise choices regarding our bodies and relationships.

Being celibate is a challenging journey, but it does become more manageable over time if approached with the right mindset. As creations of God, our natural inclinations often lead us toward visual and sensual experiences. Personally, a significant turning point for me was becoming mindful of the music I listened to. It's tough to commit to abstaining from sexual acts while constantly surrounded by songs that evoke feelings of physical intimacy. Despite my love for various music genres, I consciously decided to change my listening habits, especially when it came to R&B singers and their sensual love songs. Instead, I turned to my favorite worship leaders and gospel tunes, even though it might not seem as trendy to play those tracks in my freshly cleaned car.

However, this shift played a crucial role in cleansing my mind and soul, drawing me closer to God, which was my ultimate goal. I found this intentional time of cleansing to be incredibly fulfilling. It wasn't just about avoiding thoughts of sex, but it was driven by my genuine desire to strengthen my relationship with God. Listening to my favorite worship songs provided me with an opportunity to connect with God, talk to Him, and lay all my concerns at His feet.

Therefore, I encourage everyone to be intentional about spending time with God and entrusting all their cares to Him during this journey.

Making changes to what I listened to significantly impacted my state of mind. Consequently, I became more mindful of the television programs I watched. Ladies, let me assure you that it's not a walk in the park, and embarking on this celibacy journey has been far from easy. However, what keeps me going is the knowledge that I am dedicating myself entirely and sincerely to God. In the past, I never truly bonded with or sacrificed anything for God. I used to pick and choose which parts of myself I wanted to offer to Him. For example, I would consider attending church on Sundays as if it was enough to maintain a relationship with Him.

Knowing that I am dedicating myself to God makes life all the more meaningful. The unbreakable connection I share with God is a source of comfort and strength that no one can break or take away. Deep down, I have complete faith that when God brings my future husband into my life, during our courting phase, he will recognize that I am meant to be his wife, guided by God. Should he be the one destined for me, he will patiently await our union, cherishing the bond we share.

Being celibate requires taking certain steps, and it's not a change that happens overnight. The first crucial aspect is being certain that you genuinely want to commit to this path. Surrendering ourselves to God is a fundamental part of living a celibate life, which entails abstaining from pornography and masturbation. It is a way of offering all aspects of our being to God, given that He gave his only begotten Son to grant us eternal life. Embracing celibacy becomes a humble and obedient display of our love for God.

Admittedly, maintaining celibacy is challenging, but perseverance and hard work are necessary. To avoid temptations, it's essential to engage in productive activities that keep the mind occupied and focused. An idle mind tends to wander, leading to thoughts that might conflict with the celibate commitment. By cultivating discipline over one's thoughts and mind, it becomes possible to overcome such challenges.

On personal reflection, I acknowledge that I struggled on days when I had free time and was alone with my emotions. During these moments, thoughts about sex surfaced quite frequently. To combat such temptations, exercising immediate control over the mind is vital. Diverting focus to productive pursuits like going for a walk or hitting the gym, treating myself to a meal, and staying busy can help steer away from unhealthy thoughts.

Furthermore, maintaining a close connection with God is of utmost importance. This can be achieved through prayer, fasting, and being openly honest with God about our struggles and imperfections, which allows us to find solace and strength in our journey. It's crucial to bear in mind that perfection is not the ultimate objective; instead, it's about the continuous effort to rise above our failings and reassert our dedication to celibacy.

Stay busy and stay productive, but also hold yourself accountable as you pray and talk to God. You'll come to realize that actively seeking God and asking for His help can bring meaningful changes to your life, including the kind of friends you choose to associate with and engage in regular conversations with. The best part is, you don't have to fret about transforming your circle and environment all on your own—leave that to God. He will take care of it all and make everything fall into place for you. Trust in His plan, and you'll witness remarkable transformations in your life.

I can honestly say that I found myself feeling increasingly lonely. It seemed as though people were slowly distancing themselves from me. You know what they say: When you change and grow for the better, you don't have to remove yourself from people; they will naturally drift away from you. I began to wonder, "Doesn't anyone like me anymore? Why is no one inviting me out? Am I changing in a way that puts people off from hanging out with me?" I stopped receiving invitations to events, parties, brunches, and more. Initially, I took it very personally, and these thoughts lingered for quite some time. However, over time, I came to realize that it was not solely up to others but also a plan of God's, allowing relationships that lacked purpose to come to an end. God led me to a place where it was all about purpose and destiny, and if I didn't align with that, He guided me to walk away. Gradually, I began to accept this reality and feel okay with it. Most importantly, I reached a point where I no longer cared about the narratives others created to justify why they didn't call or stopped inviting me out. My focus shifted to embracing God's plan and finding contentment in my purpose-filled journey.

I used to have girlfriends with whom I'd have comfortable girl talks centered around sex, especially when we had a few drinks. However, since I've committed to walking the path of celibacy, I've had to change my mindset and conversations. Making immediate changes in my lifestyle became crucial to truly transform myself. If I know that having a drink might trigger sexual urges, I now exercise discipline and refrain from indulging. In the past, when hanging out with friends, alcohol often led us to discuss our past sexual encounters. But when I reflect on my life now, I can see that God has altered my environment.

The friends I have today are on the same celibacy journey, not because we made a pact, but because God brought like-minded individuals together. Our conversations are more focused on our daily lives, our work, and future business endeavors. We also pray with and for each other, and I am humbled to see how God works in such ways. When you genuinely desire positive transformation, wholeheartedly pray, ask God to reside in your heart, and express your willingness to follow His will for your life; He will undoubtedly guide you.

As my professional world flourished, so did every other aspect of my life, including my friendships. I cannot imagine navigating this journey alone. Frankly, discussions about sex rarely arise when I interact with my friends. Our conversations primarily revolve around empowering, supporting, and motivating each other to pursue our dreams and aspirations. We cherish the time we spend together, lifting one another up and providing unwavering encouragement.

Celibacy begins with a mental commitment. One of the key steps I took was to invest in myself, meaning I cleared my mind of distractions and stopped engaging in meaningless relationships. This change allowed me to redirect my focus towards personal growth and development. During my time in Louisiana, I devoted a lot of energy to my work after receiving a well-deserved promotion. I embraced the role of "being a boss" and dedicated myself to excelling in my professional life. However, I also made sure to set aside quality time for God. When I returned home, I prioritized spending time with God through prayer and reading, marking a significant milestone in my adult journey to strengthen my relationship with Christ.

What I appreciate most about my walk with God is its simplicity. The key is to have a genuine desire for change within your heart. Once you've established that, the key is to maintain a close connection with God. For me, my walk with God feels natural and organic. He holds a special place in my heart as both my ultimate love and my dearest friend. Often, we tend to overcomplicate spirituality when it comes to our relationship with God, but in reality, it doesn't have to be so profound. When I pray and have conversations with God, it's as simple and heartfelt as this:

God, I love you so much. I do not want anything that is not aligned with your will. I want you, God. I need you, God. I thank you for loving me, Father. I thank you for keeping me. I do not want to have sex with anyone other than my husband. Please help me every day to make the right decisions as it starts with me.

See, it's truly that simple. Those humble prayers in the morning and throughout the day have been a profound part of my journey. In the early stages, I found myself in tears, pouring my heart out to God. There were nights when I prayed and wept myself to sleep, overwhelmed by the immense love and protection God extends to me. Patience and waiting on God may not always come effortlessly, but the rewards of this enduring faith are undoubtedly worth the wait.

When I relocated to Texas, I felt a strong urge to deepen my relationship with Christ. Settling in Corpus Christi, I made a sincere effort to connect with like-minded, God-fearing women, and I actively searched for a church to call my spiritual home. My dedication to God was unwavering; I approached it with utmost seriousness. I vividly recall driving two hours every Sunday for a consecutive month to attend a church in San Antonio - that's how committed I was.

Reflecting on my determination, I realized that I had once driven ten hours from Chicago to Mississippi to see a boyfriend while he was in school. If I could invest that much time and effort for a person, then surely, I could do the same for God. I believe that maintaining a relationship with Christ requires effort and dedication, just like any other relationship in our lives. It's a continuous journey, and we must strive to strengthen that bond through our actions and choices.

I was incredibly focused on work and nurturing my relationship with God, leaving little room in my mind for thoughts about sex. As I mentioned earlier, I had struggled with alcoholism in the past, and to find sobriety not just for my body but also for my soul, I made the decision to give up wine and champagne entirely. I refer to this process as "Starving your distractions and feeding your focus." It required a great deal of effort, but I knew that if I wanted to improve my life, I had to put in the hard work. Admittedly, on my off days at home, my mind would sometimes wander, but I made a conscious effort to stay on track. I constantly reminded myself that to embrace the blessings God had in store for me, I had to make sacrifices and fight against my own desires. I was determined not to miss out on the abundant blessings meant for me.

In order to keep myself occupied and productive, I gave myself a pep talk and engaged in regular workouts. Additionally, I made it a daily habit to walk for an hour. The dedication to staying busy and productive paid off, and when I moved to Texas, I took it a step further by joining a gym. Every evening, I dedicated an hour to my workout routine at the gym, continuing to prioritize my personal growth and well-being.

When I relocated to Atlanta, I decided to re-enter the dating scene after a seven-year hiatus. This time around, I was certain that I was emotionally prepared and determined not to compromise my relationship with God for anyone. In the past, I had attempted celibacy even during my previous relationships, but unfortunately, I would always end up giving in sooner or later. However, my confidence was now unwavering, and I genuinely wanted to uphold the commitment I had made to God.

I remember telling myself, "If a man truly wants me, he will be willing to wait." I firmly believed that if God allowed me to find my soulmate in Atlanta, it wouldn't take long for him to recognize our connection and realize that we were meant for each other. By "not taking long," I meant that within six months of meeting, both of us should be able to decide if we want to pursue a future together because we would truly see the potential for a lasting relationship.

Celibacy has been a transformative journey for me, both mentally and spiritually. It has granted me a profound sense of freedom, liberating me from the feeling of being emotionally enslaved. I recall my days of attending church on Sundays, consistently finding myself at the altar, yearning to improve but struggling to do so on my own. At that time, I failed to recognize that I was holding on to sex, thinking I had it all under control, while hoping God would miraculously fix other aspects of my life. However, I've come to understand that such an approach is not effective. True growth and healing require a more holistic and sincere effort.

> Present your body as a living sacrifice to God. "I appeal to you therefore brothers by the mercies of God, to present your bodies as a living sacrifice, holy and acceptable to God, which is your spiritual worship" (Romans 12:1–2)

When I moved to Louisiana, I embarked on a celibacy walk, deciding not to date during that period. My intention was to bare myself before God, surrendering everything to Him – my mind, body, and time. The beginning was tough, especially since I was accustomed to having a companion, a partner, and overall comfort. It felt like going cold turkey. Nevertheless, I embraced the solitude, spending quality time with myself, engaging in prayer, and pouring out my heart to God. I cannot deny that it was a lonely journey; many nights were spent in tears, crying out to God, seeking His forgiveness, and expressing my deep desire to be closer to Him. I yearned for God's comfort and mercy, knowing that I truly wanted to become a better person through this process.

Outside of prayer and spending time with God, I kept myself occupied with various activities focused on enhancing my mental and physical well-being. As mentioned earlier, I dedicated an entire hour after work to daily walks, and I even made the decision to invest in a treadmill to maintain my fitness routine. I began to realize that life offers so much more than just focusing on sex; there are countless other fulfilling aspects to look forward to.

Taking care of my physical health became a real passion for me, and the sense of freedom it brought was incredibly rewarding. However, despite my productivity and commitment to exercise, I couldn't escape moments of loneliness. During those times, I learned to lean on and rely on God for comfort. There were nights when I found myself awake until the early hours, tearful and seeking solace from God. It was during these moments that I truly understood the desire to grow and improve as a person, acknowledging that nothing worth fighting for comes easily.

I found a healthy balance between self-care, spiritual connection, and personal growth. While challenges arose, my faith in God's guidance provided the strength to overcome them and continue on my journey of becoming a better version of myself.

When you wholeheartedly devote yourself to God, He opens doors for you. After spending nearly a year in Baton Rouge, Louisiana, an unexpected opportunity arose, and I was asked to run one of the busiest stores for the company in Texas. My focus had always been on pushing myself to excel in my career, but little did I know that God had plans in store for me. I hadn't actively sought this new opportunity; it was a result of God's guidance.

Moving to Texas turned out to be a pivotal moment in my life. It was there that I discovered my true purpose, thanks to my strong connection with God and self-awareness. My faith grew even stronger during my time in Texas. My passion for building a profound relationship with God became the priority, leading me to make choices that aligned with His teachings.

As I continued my journey in Texas, I found myself not desiring to date or let anything come between my relationship with God. My devotion to Him brought me immense joy and fulfilment, and I knew that staying true to this path was the right decision. When we surrender ourselves to God's will, remarkable opportunities and clarity about our purpose can come into our lives. Texas became a turning point for me, a place where my faith flourished, and my devotion to God's plan led me to find my true calling.

I dedicated myself to working diligently, and my efforts were recognized when I was chosen among hundreds of store directors to participate in a confidential project. This opportunity felt like a validation of my alignment with God's plan for my life. Through divine revelation, I became aware of my purpose – to inspire, motivate, encourage, and uplift young women. While I wasn't entirely sure how to manifest this calling, I was certain that it was my true vocation.

As I deepened my focus on my relationship with God, I noticed a profound shift in my mentality concerning the next steps in my life. At that moment, I couldn't quite pinpoint the exact cause, but I was certain that my thoughts had transformed due to the intentional time I spent listening to God's voice regarding my life. The unmistakable feeling in my spirit affirmed that it was time for a career change. And so, that marked the beginning of a new journey.

Once again, I found myself uncertain about what steps to take and where my path would lead, but deep within my spirit, I sensed that the time had come to search for a new job. So, I took action and began reaching out to other companies. Looking back, I believe it was God's way of preparing my mindset for the opportunities that lay ahead. With a sense of urgency, I needed to make a decision promptly.

Around the same time, my perspective on my current career and role started to shift. Unexpectedly, an old friend and former colleague reached out to me early one morning at 5 a.m. He was looking for someone interested in joining his current company as a lead executive. Without hesitation, I responded boldly, "I am!" It felt as though God had orchestrated the whole situation. It was like a revelation, guiding me through this transition period.

As I contemplate my journey, I realize that had I been entangled in a relationship or seeking physical intimacy, I might not have had the space or clarity to be open to what God had planned for me. My celibacy played a crucial role in deepening my connection with God and understanding the importance of His guidance in my life.

Even though I had to prepare for several interviews, the process went exceptionally smoothly. It seemed as though they were in awe of my qualifications and what I had to offer. A few months later, I was thrilled to receive an offer for the position and relocated to the vibrant city of Atlanta, Georgia. Moving to Atlanta turned out to be the most transformative event of my adult years, akin to surrendering myself entirely to a higher purpose. It felt like destiny had been patiently waiting for me to take this step.

God's blessings have surpassed my expectations, and I'm humbled to realize that I am not yet even fulfilling my true purpose, which is to support and mentor young women. As I continue to grow, I look forward to embracing my calling and making a meaningful impact on the lives of those around me.

Living in Atlanta and working in my gift have been truly great experiences. Just like the previous company, the current one recognized and valued my abilities and skills. I vividly recall how worried my dad was initially about the transition, fearing that my hard work might not be acknowledged. However, by the grace of God, I seamlessly adapted to my new role, and everything fell into place effortlessly. Trusting in God and surrendering all my worries to Him has been the key to my success. When you walk with God, placing all your burdens on His shoulders, He will continue to grant you the desires of your heart. Aligning yourself with His will means that your desires become aligned with His as well.

Emotionally, engaging in sex can be draining, and it may leave little room for a strong connection with God, especially when it occurs outside of marriage. Surprisingly, around 10 percent of married couples choose to wait until after marriage to have sex. Wouldn't it be amazing to be part of that 10 percent and allow God to work through you in a profound way? Embracing celibacy offers a unique opportunity to focus on your faith, personal growth, and career, leaving little time to dwell on thoughts of sex. While it's natural for such thoughts to cross your mind, being aligned with God's will becomes your ultimate priority. Celibacy is not just a temporary decision; it's a transformative lifestyle. To fully commit to celibacy, it requires a change in mentality and a complete shift in your way of living. Embracing celibacy means aligning all aspects of your life with your newfound commitment, rather than indulging in conflicting behaviors like frequent partying, drinking, and feeding your spirit by listening to negative and inappropriate music. You must change your mentality as it is a total lifestyle change.

Remember, our journey with Christ requires genuine commitment and an open heart to submit all areas of our lives to Him. It is through this surrender that we can experience His transformative power and find fulfilment in His divine purpose for us.

The transition to becoming better may not be easy. Start with small goals each day. Hold yourself accountable!

God, keep my eyes on you. I'm trying my best to become a better me—not perfect but better—and I want to work hard at it every day. As I transition to becoming better, help me to be thankful for my wins and not be disappointed in myself when things do not go as I planned. Help me to trust that if I am aligned with your will, all will be well. I pray that as I continue to challenge myself every day, you will continue to keep me accountable, and I can become the woman you called me to be.

Amen.

2

GENERATIONAL CURSES

My healing journey to becoming better.

Maintaining love to thousands, and forgiving wickedness, rebellion and sin. Yet he does not leave the guilty unpunished: he punishes the children and their children and their children for the sin of the parents to the third and fourth generation.

—Exodus 34:7 NIV

Generational curses describe the cumulative effect on a person of something our ancestors did, believed, or practiced. They are consequences of those actions, beliefs, and sins passed down through the generations.

After spending dedicated time with God, embarking on what I would call a spiritual cleanse to liberate myself from the influence of sex, I made the decision to take a pause from dating. My focus shifted towards seeking God's guidance to heal and break free from the burden of generational curses. An illustrative example of such a curse is when a fifteen-year-old girl becomes pregnant outside of wedlock. Consequently, her child, be it a daughter or son, follows the same pattern, experiencing teenage pregnancy and having a child at the age of fifteen as well. This cycle perpetuates through the generations, constituting a generational curse.

For me, breaking the cycle of mental depression, dysfunctional marriages, sexual impurity, and unhealthy family dynamics has been my utmost priority. I prayed that these issues would end with me, and I am determined not to pass them down to my children. Unfortunately, depression and various forms of mental illness have a history in my family, with both my maternal grandmother and my mother having struggled with these challenges. I vividly remember an incident during my high school years when my mother had a nervous breakdown while we were at a family reunion out of town. It was shocking to witness her hearing voices and behaving unlike herself. My mother, who used to be the nurturing figure picking me and my little brother up from school and welcoming us with hot butter cookies, suddenly took a turn for the worst. The situation led to her admission to a mental hospital where she had to stay for a couple of weeks, and it was an incredibly difficult time for all of us. This experience reinforced the significance of mental health for me. I realized that neglecting our mental well-being can lead to devastating consequences, affecting not just ourselves but our entire family. Taking care of our mental health is crucial to prevent falling apart and breaking the harmful patterns that have plagued our family history.

It is important to me that I pray for my mental state while I pray for my future husband's well-being. In the past, specifically when dealing with bad breakups, I found myself mentally crawling into a hole. Our past setbacks in life can, in fact, be passed on to us. I used to not talk to family or friends and disappear for months. I would sit at home, sleep all day, and cry myself to sleep. To break out of it, I had to pray. Instead of just crying, I had to form words out of my mouth and cry my heart out to God, asking him to heal my mind and rid me of anything that was not like him. You must check yourself and your mental health. Seeking professional help is absolutely okay and often a commendable choice. That is what many of us do wrong. We do not discuss our problems or share things that concern us. It will destroy you internally and clog your mental space.

My prayer to God is that He continues to push, guide, and support me in making the right decisions in life, while also protecting my mental well-being. I understand that many of the challenges we face are a result of our own choices, and I take responsibility for dealing with the outcomes. A verse that resonates with me is Exodus 20:5 (NIV), which serves as a warning not to repeat the mistakes of our ancestors: "You shall not bow down to them or worship them, for I, the Lord your God, am a jealous God, punishing the children for the sin of the parents to the third and fourth generation of those who hate me." I seek to learn from the past and strive to avoid perpetuating negative patterns in my life and the lives of those around me. With God's grace and wisdom, I aim to grow into a better, more virtuous person, breaking free from the destructive cycles that may have affected my family in the past.

Every day of my life, I am purposeful in my walk with Christ. My deepest desire is to have God's presence with me both in the present and throughout my future. In my prayers, I seek His divine guidance and leadership every single day. I humbly ask for forgiveness and seek His assistance in my journey. My heart earnestly yearns for the path that God has destined for me and my life. My ultimate aspiration is to align everything I do with God's will, and I wholeheartedly relinquish anything that doesn't align with His plan for me.

Reflecting on my life and past, I recognize the significant struggles I endured. My determination to fight back against challenges ultimately led to me being expelled from school. I sought solace in men for love and turned to sex for comfort, and my anger issues caused problems in my life. However, my experiences have given me a newfound perspective, and I am determined to ensure that my future daughter and nieces do not have to face the same hardships. To secure a brighter future for them, I realized the need for personal transformation. Embracing a life centered around my faith in God, I now strive to be more obedient, cultivate patience instead of quick anger, take control of my emotions, and commit to a life of celibacy. Through these positive changes, I hope to set a better example for my loved ones and pave the way for a more fulfilling and virtuous life.

If I had not made the decision to change, I would have likely ended up in a similar situation – married with children who faced the same struggles I once did. However, the remarkable aspect of this journey is that my personal growth has allowed me to become a source of true guidance for them. Now, they can overcome the same challenges that once held me back. My transformation came from placing my trust in God, relying on Him, and striving to become a better person.

It all starts with self-awareness – being fully conscious of one's own thoughts, emotions, and actions – and also being aware of our family's background. Sadly, many parents, like mine, seldom talk about their difficult pasts. As I grew older and demonstrated maturity and spiritual growth, my parents began opening up to me. Specifically, my mother and aunts shared their experiences with me.

This newfound awareness has not only allowed me to break free from the cycle of struggles but also empowered me to support and uplift future generations. It is a testament to the strength that comes from embracing change and seeking to better oneself through faith and self-discovery.

When you are fully aware of your past and possess self-awareness regarding the current personal issues you are struggling with, you gain the insight needed to understand how to approach prayer and determine what to pray for. It's essential to recognize that past struggles do not define your future, and they need not lead to failure or prevent you from achieving success in life. Embrace the decision to be resilient and opting to lead a better life by committing yourself to diligent daily efforts. With dedication and perseverance, you can overcome obstacles and create a brighter future for yourself.

I witnessed my mother's struggles while growing up, but at that time, I didn't fully grasp their potential impact on my life. Consequently, I never sought solace in prayer or talked to God about anything. However, as I matured, I began to notice aspects of my mother's traits and some of my father's struggles manifesting in my own behavior. Realizing that I wanted to break free from these patterns and strive for personal growth, I made a conscious effort to address them. One significant area of struggle for me was related to my sexuality, as I am aware of my sensuality and the temptations that lead me astray. To pursue a righteous path, I decided to embrace celibacy and commit to a godly marriage, where God would be the cornerstone of our union, guiding us away from sinful thoughts and adultery. I knew that for a successful marriage, it was crucial not to carry these negative spirits into it, and so, I made the choice to change for the better.

One of the challenges I faced in my journey with sexuality was the decision to refrain from dating while undergoing a spiritual cleanse. Contrary to the belief that you can only find a partner if you're actively out there searching, I hold a different perspective. Living a life fully devoted to God, my activities and priorities may differ. Currently, my main focus is on my current project, A Better You, which aligns with my purpose. Alongside my career, I also prioritize self-care, both physically and mentally. Regular visits to the gym, occasional travels, treating myself to dinners, and enjoying spa sessions are some ways I nurture myself. I've let go of the pressure to actively pursue dating; instead, I'm open to the possibility of it happening naturally and organically. Considering that mental illness runs in my family, I'm proactive about self-awareness and regularly checking in on my mental well-being. If I notice myself pushing people away or isolating myself, I make a deliberate effort to spend quality time with friends and family, as their support is essential for my overall happiness and growth.

You must always check yourself and avoid dwelling in self-pity. I have actively chosen not to embrace failure and instead, I work diligently each day. Being a go-getter is an inherent trait in my personality. We've talked about the bad, so let me brag about the good. My father holds a prestigious position as a highly intelligent Chief Compliance Officer in a Fortune 100 company, while my mother graduated as the valedictorian, ranking at the top of her class. It is in my blood to strive for greatness, especially with the numerous successful aunts, uncles, and cousins in my family. Among them are educators, including my uncle who serves as the Deputy Chief of the Chicago Police, as well as executive directors of technology, Secret Service agents, scientists, architects, nurses, and doctors – the list goes on. Greatness runs in my veins, and I made the conscious choice to embrace as I pursued the journey of becoming better.

I chose to push myself to greatness. The funny thing is, unlike some of my friends in high school, I didn't have my life meticulously mapped out. As a high school senior, while my friends had various college options to choose from, I felt lost. One lunchtime during the fourth quarter of our senior year, I remember everyone excitedly discussing the colleges they were accepted to, while I felt embarrassed and inadequate. The truth is, my first two years of high school were a struggle. I was unfocused, and my academic performance suffered. While I don't want to solely blame my mother's mental state, it undoubtedly played a significant role in the challenges I faced. Her condition had a profound impact on me and my ability to concentrate on schoolwork. With my mom, unable to provide daily check-ins after school and my dad working tirelessly to support the family, I often felt like I was navigating life alone. As a young teenager dealing with so much, including my mother's illness and her being in a mental institution, I was hurting and lost, unsure how to cope without her by my side. Consequently, my academic performance suffered.

However, I am grateful for the favor and grace bestowed upon me by God, providing me with an opportunity to turn my life around. I realized I needed to change, and I started working hard every day to make positive improvements. I'll forever be thankful to God for entrusting me with the life He has blessed me with, giving me the strength to overcome adversity and work towards a better future.

Breaking generational curses is a profound and transformative journey. Recently, I experienced a breakthrough by finding the strength to forgive my father. Through seeking God and listening to His voice, I gained a new perspective. I came to understand that people can only be what they know how to be, and I had been expecting something from my father that he could not provide—not because he didn't want to, but because he was occupied with work and the responsibility of providing for our family. During my teenage years, he was the only mentally stable family member I had. However, when I needed his support the most, he seemed unable to fully understand and address my needs. At the time, I couldn't see that he was also dealing with my mother's illness and coping with it the best way he knew how.

Unfortunately, I held onto resentment and anger for a long time, unable to see the situation from his perspective. But one day, during a moment of self-reflection in front of the mirror, I had an awakening. I realized that I needed to make a change and consciously decided to stop blaming my actions and personality on the absence of my parents' active involvement in my life. Taking responsibility, I chose to forge my own path and not let past circumstances define who I am or how I live my life. This decision to let go of bitterness and embrace forgiveness has been liberating, empowering me to break free from the chains of generational patterns and create a positive future for myself. It's an ongoing journey, but I am now determined to move forward with love, understanding, and a newfound sense of self.

Reflecting back, there was a time when I relied on what I knew best: working hard until success was achieved. I firmly believe in the principle that God rewards effort and dedication, not just mere wishes. This guiding principle has been a constant force in my life and continues to shape my journey. Although I didn't have a concrete plan for my ideal job, I remained committed to giving my best effort in everything I pursued.

During my tenure as a cashier at a Fortune 100 retailer, I pushed myself to be the fastest and most efficient in my role. Whether it was handling transactions or processing returns, I strived to excel in every aspect of my work. It was during this time that my dedication caught someone's attention, leading to a well-deserved promotion to checkout supervisor.

With my new position, my determination to be the best only grew stronger. I embraced the motto, "I am not replaceable," rejecting the notion of interchangeability among individuals. When I encountered the phrase, "We are all replaceable," I couldn't help but disagree, recognizing the unique set of skills and qualities that I bring to the table on all levels. Some might view this mindset as arrogance, but I attribute it to embracing how I believe God created me. I firmly believe that I am irreplaceable, and I remind myself of this empowering fact each and every day.

After putting in considerable effort and excelling as a supervisor, I earned a well-deserved promotion to assistant store manager. Interestingly, my career path wasn't meticulously planned; instead, I focused on giving my best every day, and eventually, the opportunity presented itself. Hard work seems to be an inherent trait in my family, passed down through generations; my grandfather was a successful businessman, and my father was often referred to as a workaholic. It's simply ingrained in us. However, amidst moments of leisure and even on my days off, I noticed a concerning pattern of depression and anxiety surfacing.

One day, while living in Chicago, I found myself driving to a friend's house when an unexpected wave of emotions hit me. Tears began streaming down my face uncontrollably, far from the cute tears I had experienced before. In that moment of vulnerability, I instinctively reached out to my beloved aunty, whom I am eternally grateful for having in my life. As I poured my heart out to her, the strange thing was, I couldn't pinpoint exactly what was wrong. It was as if the weight of my emotions had become too overwhelming for me to comprehend, leaving me unable to put it into words. I had been so engrossed in my work, deliberately avoiding confronting the realities of my life.

As previously mentioned, I had a well-paying job, earning a comfortable six-figure income, yet my living situation was anything but ideal. Despite my financial success, I found myself sleeping on a sofa chair in my aunt's bedroom. On top of that, I had been dealing with the challenges of having a mother who was struggling with mental illness, adding another layer of complexity to my already burdened heart. And to make matters worse, the pain from a past failed relationship continued to haunt me, leaving me heartbroken and unable to fully heal.

In that moment of vulnerability, I realized I needed to confront these issues and allow myself the space to process my emotions. It was time to acknowledge the impact of these circumstances on my well-being and find a way to heal and grow. With the support of my aunty and a newfound determination, I embarked on a journey of self-discovery, seeking healing and personal transformation.

Let's begin with the deep sense of internal brokenness I carried, shielding my heart from processing the emotions surrounding my mother's illness. Throughout my younger years, and even into my teenage and adult life, my closest friends had the privilege of turning to their mothers for support, whether it was getting ready for their first dances or seeking a confidant during tough times. Unlike them, I didn't have that luxury. There was no mother to remind me that I looked beautiful every day, to embrace me and express her love, or to listen eagerly as I excitedly shared stories about my first crush or boyfriend. These seemingly simple moments held immense significance, and the absence of them left a void in my life. Some of you reading this may relate, having experienced the love and guidance of a mother figure. Just envision how different life would be if you couldn't simply call your mommy to seek her opinion on preparing a roast, greens, or lasagna?

Life was a journey I had to navigate on my own, and in that process, I discovered the incredible nature of God. His boundless favor and mercy became evident as I went through various experiences as a young woman, ultimately leading me to a profound connection with Him. Learning to lean on God for love, guidance, and nurturance was a transformative experience. Through prayer and introspection, I came to understand the importance of protecting my unborn child, my daughter, from the hardships and pain I had endured during my own childhood. Witnessing my mother's struggles and brokenness, I vowed to shield my daughter from similar mental anguish and suffering. My deepest desire is to create a different, nurturing environment, one where she can grow and flourish without being weighed down by my past wounds.

If I allowed myself to remain in that dark space, things would have only worsened. I found myself crying without any clear explanation for my emotions. I felt discontented with both myself and my position in life, and the overwhelming sensation was one of brokenness. Recognizing the need for change, I made the decision to step out of that darkness and begin the healing process. But how does one heal? For me, it began with creating a protective bubble around myself and my peace of mind. I turned to prayer as a means to address the feelings I harbored towards my mother and the unfulfilled relationship I believed we should have had. Through prayer, I sought not only my own healing but also for my mother's well-being, her mind, and her heart. Although immediate changes were not evident in my mother's behavior, I had to accept that fact and find solace in trusting God and the healing process itself.

I had what I would call "mommy issues" - yes, the term may sound unconventional, but it accurately describes the emotional struggles I faced during my teenage years. Throughout that period, I was going through life, but I never truly delved into my feelings about my mother. Surprisingly, it wasn't until my adult years that I came to recognize these issues.

My journey towards healing began when I relocated to Louisiana, not solely because of the city or state, but because it provided me with an environment where I could learn and discover my true identity as a woman and as a child of God. The process of self-discovery was both enlightening and transformative.

Having a mother figure can be nurturing, and it is crucial for mothers to raise their children with utmost care and affection. As a mother, you hold the responsibility of providing both physical and emotional support to your children, fostering a strong and healthy bond with them.

When I was fourteen years old, my mom suffered from depression, and during that period, I needed her support the most. At fifteen years old, starting high school was a daunting experience without having my mom to confide in when I came home. The first two years of high school were undoubtedly torturous. As I grew older, I realized that I struggled to accept love from women, not because of any intentional resistance, but simply because I didn't know how to. I had built up emotional walls, making it difficult for me to open up and trust others.

Healing from my experiences with my mom is a journey that I continue to work on diligently every day. The process began with earnest prayers and a conscious effort to seek God's guidance and protection for my mind and heart. It's crucial to acknowledge that God plays a pivotal role in our lives, and His power to work miracles should not be underestimated. By actively seeking God daily, I have come to realize the profound impact it can have on my healing.

A significant part of my recovery also involved letting go of any resentment or envy towards the close relationships I observed between my cousins and their moms or my friends and their mothers. Instead of letting frustration consume me, I chose to channel my energy into showing more love and appreciation towards my own mom. Every day, I make a point of praying for her and seeking God's blessings and intervention on her behalf.

Healing from generational curses has been challenging but deeply rewarding. I am learning to trust in God's plan and find comfort in His presence as I continue to grow and overcome the difficulties from my past experiences with my mom.

I decided to break the cycle of mental illness within my family, making a conscious choice that it would end with me. This decision stemmed from my awareness of both my own past and my family's history. While my mother's struggles with mental health could have affected me, I was determined that they would not define my life. Instead of succumbing to self-pity and blaming my upbringing for any poor decisions I might have made, I took a different path. I resolved to strive for self-improvement and personal growth, recognizing that change had to start from within.

Given the hereditary nature of mental illness in my family, I could have easily allowed myself to be consumed by that sense of brokenness. However, I chose a different course. I confronted my pain and experiences head-on, finding strength in understanding my childhood and actively seeking healing through prayer and self-reflection.

I encourage others to do the same. Embrace your past, acknowledge the pain it may have caused, and actively seek ways to change and grow. Remember, we have the power to shape our destinies and break free from the limitations that may have been handed down to us. By tapping into our own hurts, we can find the strength to overcome them and create a brighter future for ourselves and our loved ones.

People often perceive me as the golden child or the favorite, but little do they know that I struggled terribly with mommy and daddy issues. Realizing and acknowledging our hurts, struggles, and shortcomings is crucial, as it allows us to actively pray about them and seek guidance regularly. Healthy family dynamics hold great importance for me. During my younger years, my mom fell ill, and although my dad did an excellent job providing for the family, I felt emotionally neglected. As a result, I became accustomed to being alone and developed a preference for solitude. This trait is shared with my sister, and together, we learned to rely solely on ourselves, not counting on or leaning on anyone else. Growing up with my mom's illness, it was just the three of us—my brother, sister, and me.

When I reflect on the past, I now realize that some people were unaware of the gravity of my mother's illness. Had they known, perhaps they would have checked in on my siblings and me. However, it's possible that everyone was dealing with their own life issues and couldn't provide the emotional support we needed. Consequently, we had to navigate those challenges on our own. Now, as an adult, I make a conscious effort to ensure my nieces and nephews know me well. I cherish the role of being their Aunty, and I want them to feel comfortable reaching out to me whenever they need anything. Family holds immense importance in my life.

During my childhood, I shared a close bond with my cousins and siblings, but I yearned for adult guidance, love, and emotional support. Therefore, I strive to be that source of support for my nieces and nephews now. It brings a smile to my face every time my nephew sends me a text expressing his love or asking for fifteen dollars on his cash app to buy a video game. He knows I am his Aunty, and I cherish that connection.

My seven-year-old niece also adores her Aunty and feels at ease talking to me. I want her to know that if, for any reason, she can't turn to her parents, I will be there for her. She has her Aunty as a pillar of support in her life.

When my mother fell ill, it was just the three of us - a fourteen-year-old, a twelve-year-old, and a seven-year-old. On the surface, it might have appeared that everything was perfect, but the reality was far from it. My sister had to grow up without a mom, transitioning from a seven-year-old to an adult without her guiding presence. Though I tried my best to be a good big sister, there were times when I was emotionally absent. I longed for the nurturing and support I needed myself, which unfortunately led me to unintentionally neglect my sister and project my own feelings of inadequacy onto her. All of us yearned for our mother, but her mental condition prevented her from providing us with what we truly needed. I have friends who grew up without their parents, but fortunately, they had other family members who stepped in and closed the gap. In contrast, my family, including my aunts and uncles, tried their best, but we often felt isolated and alone. Regular check-ins or someone sitting with us while we did our homework to ensure we were okay, were rare occurrences. It's essential to acknowledge that they loved and cared about us, but there was a level of emotional support missing. In fact, it wasn't until my early adult years that I truly became close to my aunts and uncles. It seemed that they were unable to extend a helping hand to us, possibly due to their struggles in dealing with their sister's illness, compounded by the challenges their mother faced with her own mental health. It's possible that they were unsure of how to provide us with the support we needed, and they genuinely did their best with the resources they had at hand.

Breaking generational curses is of utmost importance as it helps prevent lingering hurt, pain, or trauma from impacting our lives. Awareness of our family history is crucial, as these issues can manifest without us realizing it. Establishing a strong spiritual foundation in God is vital to safeguard against such negative influences. It's essential to remember that our family's history of mental illness does not define us or determine our future. With unwavering faith and determination, I firmly resist the enemy's ongoing attacks on my family. Now, I stand liberated from all generational curses, empowered to shape my destiny positively. In Jesus's name, I declare this victorious transformation.

Generational curses can be passed from one generation to the next. There is nothing to be ashamed and embarrassed about. I am aware of the broken dynamics my family went through. I'm healing and trusting God to break each curse one by one.

God, please help me to understand the reason
I went through what I went through. It wasn't
by happenstance. I had to go through tough
experiences, not just for me, but so others can
grow from my mistakes. I went through what
I went through so my children don't have to
experience it and loved ones can learn from it.
Father God, as I overcome my strongholds, keep
me secure with who I am as a woman, to trust
that my past is a part of who I am and that you're
molding me into the woman you called me to be.

Amen.

3

HEALING FROM HURT CAUSED BY SELF-SABOTAGE

Immediately after healing is growth.

Create in me a pure heart, O God, and renew a steadfast spirit within me. Do not cast me from your presence or take your Holy Spirit from me. Restore to me the joy of your salvation and grant me a willing spirit, to sustain me. Then I will teach transgressors your ways, so that sinners will turn back to you.

—Psalm 51:10–13 NIV

Healing from past pain or traumatic experiences is not a quick process; it requires time, patience, dedication, and a commitment to change. While I can't speak for everyone, some women may have a tendency to seek ways to feel good and avoid feeling bad, which can lead to putting ourselves in sabotaging circumstances. Unfortunately, this often triggers self-destructive behaviors as a misguided attempt to shield ourselves from pain. By self-sabotaging, I mean exposing myself to situations that have caused me heartache and pain in the past.

> But he was wounded for our transgressions, he was bruised for our iniquities, the chastisement of our peace was upon him and with his stripes we are healed. (Isaiah 53:5 NIV)

With God's stripes, we find healing! Only by embracing God's love, protection, and covering can we prevent much of the brokenness and issues we encounter. True healing requires us to confront reality honestly, especially concerning our pasts. We must resist the temptation to conceal our imperfections and pretend that everything is perfect when it's not. Speaking from my own experience, my family, like many others, excelled at presenting a flawless exterior while hiding our brokenness within. Though unintended, that was how we were wired.

Now, let me be completely transparent. As mentioned before, women are often wired to seek pleasure and avoid discomfort, leading to self-sabotaging behaviors. Repeatedly, I found myself making poor decisions because I was broken and hurting. Yet, I believe that with God's grace, I can overcome these challenges and find true healing. By embracing God's love and acknowledging my vulnerabilities, I can grow into a stronger, wiser person."

As a teenager, I found myself in a state of brokenness, loneliness, and vulnerability. My mother struggled with mental illness, while my father was constantly preoccupied with work, solely focused on being the family provider. These circumstances led me down a path where I sought love and validation in all the wrong places.

When I was fifteen years old, I entered into a relationship with a guy, and while I must admit that "hate" is a strong word, my dad certainly had strong negative feelings towards him. Nonetheless, my dad believed in giving his children the freedom to make their own decisions, hoping that we would ultimately make the right ones. Consequently, I continued to date this guy, and three years later, I found myself pregnant at the age of eighteen while working at a call center in Chicago. Naturally, I kept the pregnancy hidden from my family, though I'm not entirely sure how I managed to do so. There were likely some suspicions from my aunts, uncles, and cousins, and even my parents were curious. I often battled with morning sickness, and around the fourth month, my dad caught me vomiting in the bathroom after an hour. Concerned, he asked me, "What's going on, baby? A stomach virus shouldn't last for weeks, and you've been throwing up for weeks now." He briefly glanced at my stomach and then walked away. "I replied, 'I just don't feel well.' I immediately left the bathroom and rushed to my room. In my heart, I knew I couldn't go through with the pregnancy. The guy I was dating was involved in drug dealing on the streets, and I knew he wasn't the right partner for me. Deep down, I understood that. The only reason I found myself four months pregnant was because he desired a baby and was excited about it. He happily shared the news with his parents. However, for me, I felt nothing but fear and unhappiness."

I knew I had to make a difficult decision and make it quickly, so I ultimately chose to terminate my pregnancy. It's a memory that still haunts me, vivid as if it happened yesterday. My boyfriend and I woke up with heavy hearts and decided to take the train downtown. Entering the facility, I couldn't help but feel a sense of shame and guilt. The nurse solemnly informed me that if I had waited just one more day, termination wouldn't have been an option due to how far along I was. Reflecting on that moment, I couldn't help but chastise myself for allowing the situation to unfold that way.

Being there was an agonizing experience. Every step was deliberately taken to ensure that I made the "right" decision. Nothing was hurried, and we spent considerable time filling out paperwork. Later, I was directed to a room where I met with another nurse who showed me a sonogram of my unborn child. Left alone in that room for what felt like an eternity, I clutched the ultrasound image in my hand while reading yet another document that encouraged me to embrace motherhood and the wonders of being a mother. As much as I wanted to, I knew I couldn't keep the baby. The reality was that I could barely afford to take care of myself, let alone provide for a child. When the nurse returned, she asked me once more for my final decision, making sure I was absolutely certain. And with a heavy heart, I answered yes.

I was escorted to another room and asked to lie down. Soon after, I was put under anesthesia. When I woke up, I found myself in a state of shock as I noticed a puddle of blood around me. The medical staff urgently urged me not to look and helped me onto a wheelchair. I was taken to the waiting room, where other women were also waiting. When the time came to leave, the staff handed me a brown bag containing a week's supply of pain medication and some crackers.

When I arrived at my boyfriend's house, overwhelmed by emotions, I couldn't contain my feelings. I collapsed into tears and curled up into a ball, consumed by grief. Losing my baby left me feeling hollow, as if a significant part of me had vanished. The weight of guilt, anger, regret, and shame bore down on me, making it difficult to cope. Subsequently, I started withdrawing from others, isolating myself, and struggling with self-esteem problems, which led to weight gain. I found myself broken, trapped in a dark and desolate place.

While I do not personally encourage choosing abortion for any woman, I must acknowledge that having unprotected sex at the age of eighteen was a self-sabotaging decision on my part. It was a choice that led to additional pain and put me in a difficult position at such a young age. At that time, I was already dealing with the challenges of my mom's mental illness, and finding myself pregnant and making the decision to terminate the pregnancy added further complexity to an already challenging situation.

As mentioned earlier, women sometimes find themselves inadvertently sabotaging their own progress by prioritizing temporary pleasure and the pursuit of immediate gratification. I can relate to this personally, as I fell into the trap of self-sabotage by prioritizing short-term pleasure over long-term well-being. My decision to engage in premarital sex, while driven by the desire for temporary pleasure, led me to face an unexpected and challenging situation. Regrettably, this focus on fleeting satisfaction ended up sabotaging my plans and resulted in an unplanned pregnancy.

If I could do it all over again, I would have made a different choice regarding practicing safe sex. Instead, I now believe that keeping my virginity for my future husband aligns with my personal values and beliefs. I have come to understand that abstaining from sex before marriage is important to me, as it reflects my commitment to a traditional and meaningful relationship. I've learned that it's essential to honor my values and not feel pressured by societal norms or expectations. By making this decision, I am embracing the idea that sex is a sacred and intimate bond meant to be shared with someone special in the context of marriage:

> Do not conform to the pattern of this world, but be transformed by the renewing of your mind. (Romans 12:2 NIV)

I told myself I was going to wait until I was married before deciding to have sex. However, I couldn't stick to that decision, and I ended up not waiting. The good news is that my boyfriend and I eventually broke up. We came to realize that we were simply too different. He was involved in selling drugs on the street, while I had outgrown the desire to be associated with the lifestyle of having a street-affiliated boyfriend.

So what did I do next? I found myself in a tumultuous, on-again-off-again relationship with a guy I had worked with for ten long years. Looking back, I can't help but feel like I invested so much time and energy into something that ultimately didn't lead to a fulfilling outcome. It's disheartening to realize that a decade of my life seems to have gone to waste. I can't help but recognize that I continuously put myself in situations where I unwittingly sabotage my own happiness and growth. It's time for some serious self-reflection and to make positive changes moving forward.

This relationship lasted a full eight years before he revealed that he no longer wanted to play games. He expressed his desire to leave behind his past with multiple other women and expressed his wish to spend the rest of his life with me. However, I made the mistake of believing him despite his history of repeatedly cheating on me with multiple women. Despite my values as a Christian woman, which advocates waiting for marriage before living with a man, we still decided to move in together. At that moment, love clouded my judgment, or at least, what I perceived to be love. He seemed to change and finally fulfill all the things I had wanted from him over the years – he chose me.

That he did, but he did not choose only me. After living together for over a year, our relationship took a negative turn as he stopped coming home at reasonable hours, leading me to suspect that he might be involved with someone else. So, how did I react? I must admit, I went through the phone records to check the numbers he was calling and texting, examining call durations and timestamps. Taking it a step further, I bravely called those numbers to see who would answer. One daring person openly confessed to being with my partner the previous night and provided a detailed description of his outfit as evidence. She described the clothing down to the exact details.

We fought and resorted to physical altercations on more than one occasion. It was a much-needed wake-up call, forcing me to confront myself in the mirror and question, "What are you doing, Candace?" Throughout my life, I had never allowed anyone to demean, humiliate, or lay a hand on me. After enduring a tumultuous on-again-off-again relationship for ten years, I finally mustered the strength to make the tough decision to leave.

As I began packing up, reality hit me hard—I had nowhere to go. Despite my success, being in my early thirties and earning a six-figure salary, I found myself homeless. Technically, I could afford a place, but the situation arose because I had moved in with a man who wasn't my husband. It was a harsh lesson to learn, and I realized that I needed to rebuild my life from scratch.

With newfound determination, I embarked on a journey of self-discovery and empowerment. Simultaneously, I focused on my career and personal growth, using my past experiences as stepping stones for learning and becoming stronger.

Life's hardships taught me the immense value of self-respect and the importance of making choices that align with my core values. I grasped that success isn't solely about financial accomplishments but also hinges on maintaining healthy relationships and prioritizing self-care. Though the road ahead was daunting, I embraced the challenges and resolved to create a brighter, more secure future for myself—one defined by resilience, courage, and a renewed sense of self-worth.

Thank God my aunt opened her door to me when I needed a place to stay. I was feeling hurt and broken-hearted, already burdened by unresolved issues with my parents, and I had ended up in another unhealthy relationship. As a result, my mental and emotional state became unstable. Reflecting on the situation, I realize there were better choices I could have made. I should have prioritized myself, opted for celibacy, and most importantly, refrained from moving in with someone I wasn't married to. These decisions would have spared me a lot of heartache, pain, and tears.

Admittedly, being single can be challenging, but its experience depends on your approach. In the past, I believed that being in a live-in situation was the essence of life. However, with hindsight, I now realize that the person I was with was unkind, unfaithful, disloyal, and dishonest. If I could turn back time, I would have chosen to place my faith in God and prioritize my well-being above all else.

In my thirties, life is absolutely wonderful. I am in great health, thriving in my career, and most importantly, I have a strong sense of my identity as a woman. This transformation came about because I made two crucial choices - to embrace God and to prioritize myself.

Consequently, I am committed to avoiding self-sabotage and any situations that could lead to harm.

Addressing my self-sabotaging tendencies required making immediate decisions. Healing is a gradual process, and while some may seek counseling, I found solace and strength in my faith in God. Over the past 8 years, I have dedicated myself to healing and achieving emotional well-being. My determination is not to let the wounds of my childhood affect my relationships. Although there are still aspects I'm working on, the advantage lies in being fully aware of the areas where growth is needed and understanding where they stem from.

Healing began with embracing pure isolation—an intentional state of being separate from others and separating myself from distractions. [Oxford Dictionary] To truly hear from God, I needed to tune out all other voices. Despite invitations to hang out or attend events, I had to decline and prioritize my time with God, seeking clarity and guidance from Him. My commitment to healing meant dedicating myself to spending quality, intentional time with God so that my healing could be lasting. For me, this involved lighting candles, indulging in a hot bubble bath, and meditating on God's Word. As I immersed myself in His teachings, I discovered a profound love for the woman God created in me, and I began to see myself through the lens of Christ. Although the journey of isolation was challenging, the rewards were immeasurable—a deep and nurturing relationship with Christ. While nobody desires to be alone, this major adjustment allowed me to cultivate a meaningful and transformative connection with Him.

I began the process of reflecting on my past, encompassing my childhood and young-adult years. It became essential for me to acknowledge the pain and hurt I had experienced and to allow God to facilitate my healing. From my earliest days as a little girl, I found myself an outcast due to the color of my skin and the texture of my hair. Without a mother figure to provide reassurance about my beauty and offer encouragement, I carried that hurt with me to school, where it manifested in negative ways. My emotional turmoil led me to connect with young women who harbored ill intentions towards me and did not prioritize my well-being.

During my time away at school, I had the opportunity to meet someone who profoundly impacted my life. The moment I encountered her, it was as if we were destined to be lifelong friends. Her beauty was evident, but what struck me most was her incredible intelligence. I saw reflections of myself in her, and I deeply admired her authenticity and ability to be true to herself. Her genuineness had a positive influence on me, inspiring me to embrace and be proud of my own identity. Since then, I have lived my life unapologetically, and anyone who knows me as Candace can attest to this fact.

It was during orientation that we truly bonded, bringing together two young, beautiful queens from Chicago, who ultimately became roommates and shared a profound connection and became roommates in college.

Self-sabotage refers to the harmful patterns that hinder personal growth and prevent individuals from achieving their full potential. [Oxford Dictionary] These self-destructive behaviors can manifest in various aspects of life, such as relationships, career, and overall well-being. Whether it's procrastination, negative self-talk, fear of failure, or succumbing to self-doubt, self-sabotage can be a formidable obstacle on the path to success and happiness. Recognizing and addressing these patterns is crucial for breaking free from the limitations they impose and creating a more fulfilling life. By fostering self-awareness, practicing self-compassion, and cultivating positive habits, individuals can gradually overcome self-sabotage and empower themselves to pursue their goals and aspirations with renewed confidence and determination.

On a foggy afternoon, my friend and I were strolling to class when we encountered a group of girls who had formed a barrier, blocking our path. Determined to get through, I managed to find a way past them. However, as I continued a few steps ahead, I noticed my friend had stopped. Frustrated and upset, she dropped her book bag and exclaimed, "I've had enough of them, Candace." As a loyal supporter, I empathized with her frustration and decided to show my solidarity by also placing my book bag down and joining her in confronting the situation.

What could I have done differently? Instead of throwing down my book bag, I should have kept it on and tried to defuse the situation. I could have also tried to restrain my friend and persuade her not to fight. Unfortunately, that's not how things unfolded. I made the impulsive decision to throw my bag down and follow my friend into the altercation. My intention was to break up the fight, but as I intervened, a young girl unexpectedly punched me in the head. The situation quickly escalated, and a sizable crowd gathered to watch, numbering around a hundred people, including highschool students who were visiting the campus that day. They taunted me, asking if I was going to let her hit me. In response, I found myself unable to back down and engaged in a fight with the girl. It only lasted about a minute before campus administrators rushed over in disappointment. This incident was especially embarrassing as there were students from ten different high schools and ten school buses present, all witnessing the commotion at the campus library's front bridge.

We were all taken to the campus courtroom, where we were promptly handed a seven-day suspension. Eventually, the college authorities reached the decision to suspend us. Reflecting on my actions, I can't help but feel foolish for getting into a fight and ending up kicked out of college. It's just another painful example of self-sabotage. Looking back, I realize that the whole situation could have been easily avoided with better choices.

Accountability is fundamentally rooted in being responsible for fulfilling one's duties and obligations. In the context of godly accountability, it entails acknowledging and taking responsibility for one's actions, while actively choosing to seek God's wisdom to discern and accomplish what is morally right. Embracing godly accountability fosters a deeper sense of integrity and spiritual growth, as it aligns our actions with higher principles and values. By allowing God to guide us, we cultivate a stronger connection with our beliefs and purpose, leading to more purposeful and virtuous lives.

If I were truly walking with God and allowing Him to be the head of my life, things would be significantly different. Unfortunately, I find myself frequently overwhelmed by fear of God. Nevertheless, my deepest passion is to embody an authentic example of who God is, constantly striving to place Him at the forefront of all my actions and decisions.

When you live a life fully devoted to God, accountability becomes a crucial aspect. It involves holding yourself in high regard and ensuring that you align with God's commandments. Personally, I have learned how to manage my emotions, avoid being easily angered, and practice thoughtfulness before speaking. This daily discipline of thinking positively has contributed significantly to my healing process. Often, the challenges we face are a result of poor decisions we've made, which essentially amounts to self-sabotage. Taking responsibility for our actions is essential in overcoming these obstacles.

I was employed at a Fortune 100 company, and during that period, I held the position of an assistant manager at one of Chicago's busiest locations. At the time, I was young, confident, and proud of my achievements as a black woman. However, with hindsight, I can see that my downfall was my lack of humility. I distinctly recall a meeting with my team to address performance concerns, and unfortunately, I concluded it with an inappropriate statement: "You see that black Cadillac outside? Well, by the looks of things, I need my job. I will not allow you all to take that away from me." Reflecting on it now, I realize how foolish and insensitive it was to say that to a group of middle-aged team members. As a leader, I should have set a much better example.

While I was recognized as a prominent leader both within my location and throughout the company, humility was not a virtue I embraced at that time. I excelled at my job, but I failed to recognize the importance of humility in leadership. Looking back on this experience, I am committed to learning from my mistakes and growing as a leader who values humility and understands its significance in fostering a supportive and effective team environment.

Nevertheless, my cockiness and arrogance finally caught up with me. I believed I was untouchable, but my store manager made the difficult decision to terminate my employment. While I acknowledge that I brought value as a leader, I also must admit that I was not always the easiest person to work with. My arrogance overshadowed my true potential, and that led to my downfall. I can't deny that I sometimes displayed favoritism towards those who flattered me, and I recognize that my behavior may have intimidated and caused jealousy among my colleagues.

In hindsight, I understand that my termination was a consequence of my own actions, and I had to come to terms with it. The experience left me feeling lost and empty, uncertain about my next steps in life. Questions swirled in my mind: What do I do now? Where should I go from here?

However, I found solace in my faith and belief in God. In moments when the world seemed unforgiving, I discovered that God's grace and favor still shone upon me, especially when I approached with a heart of repentance.

With this newfound realization, I am committed to learning from my mistakes and becoming a better person. I want to grow into a more compassionate and humble individual, showing kindness and understanding to others. While I can't change the past, I can use this experience as a catalyst for personal growth and self-improvement.

Moving forward, I hope to find new opportunities to contribute positively and meaningfully, not just as a leader but also as a team player who fosters a harmonious and supportive work environment. I understand that true strength lies in humility, and I am determined to embrace this virtue wholeheartedly.

I accept responsibility for my actions, and I am on a journey to become a better version of myself, guided by my faith and the desire to treat others with kindness and respect.

God shows us favor when we express remorse over our sins when guilt consumes us to the point of conviction. When we confess with our mouths that Jesus is Lord and believe in our hearts that God raised him from the dead, you will be saved (Romans 10:9 NIV).

I felt terrible. "Candace, out of all people, you know God. How could you put yourself in a position where you end up without a job?" I asked myself. During my time off, I confronted my shortcomings and challenged myself to reflect on my actions. I deeply questioned my integrity, and above all, I sought forgiveness. I have always prided

A Better You Experience

myself on being honest, and my integrity means everything to me. However, my own arrogance and overconfidence led me to sabotage my growing career. It was then that God intervened. Yes, with His favor, I was eventually rehired after six long months of unemployment. During my time at home, I earnestly repented not only for my professional mistakes but also for any wrongdoings in other aspects of my life. After being back in my job for a little over a year, I was unexpectedly offered a role as a store manager. I knew I didn't deserve this opportunity, but God blessed me and put His trust in me.

Life is a dynamic journey, shaped by our choices, both positive and negative. Overcoming the damage inflicted by self-sabotage has been a gradual process for me, spanning many years. I often questioned the necessity of subjecting myself to heartache and pain when life already brings its fair share of challenges. Yet, what has been truly empowering is the boundless love and support of God, unwavering even amidst our flaws and imperfections. As women, we are inherently born into a state of imperfection, grappling with our own struggles. For me, the pursuit of healing has been a profound calling. However, it remains an ongoing journey, with each day presenting opportunities for growth and improvement. Acknowledging the need for change and aspiring to be a better version of myself was the pivotal initial step towards healing, albeit a daunting one. Along the way, I found myself ensnared in a dark and difficult place, one that I could only navigate with the guidance of God. The quest for healing begins with opening your heart to God, seeking forgiveness for our transgressions, and inviting divine presence into our lives.

Healing, for me, has been a journey that took me back to my younger self - a little girl struggling to cope with anger and its origin. As I gradually discovered the source of my anger, I turned to prayer

— 57 —

and fasting to overcome those struggles. One of the most beautiful aspects of healing is that it extends beyond ourselves; it positively impacts those who will come after us, like our sisters, cousins, nieces, and nephews. I feel incredibly blessed to be an aunt and a godly example for my nieces, guiding them on the path of righteousness.

Healing is an integral part of personal growth. Understanding the reasons behind our behavior and past experiences allows us to evolve as individuals. I realized that my past should not define my present or my future. I questioned myself - how long would I allow my brokenness to hinder me from moving forward? It became clear that I could not progress without healing from my past wounds.

Choosing to heal means letting go of the burdens we carry. We must acknowledge that things won't magically disappear on their own. Embracing vulnerability and expressing our pain are essential steps in the healing process. Taking full responsibility for our actions and mistakes empowers us to make positive changes in our lives.

Above all, healing is about living in the present and finding joy in our journey. It requires a conscious decision to focus on personal growth and embrace the happiness that life has to offer. Letting go of the past allows us to flourish and truly experience life to the fullest.

Life naturally has its bumps in the road. There will be hurdles and delays. It's what you do with them and how you handle them that matters in the end! If it burns, let it burn! Let God mold you!

Through the pain and the tears, I am going to trust
you, God. Yes, I made mistakes, but I know you
are a forgiving God, and you love me. You want to
see me reach my full potential. God, heal my heart.
Help me to stay focused and keep my eyes on you.
As I navigate through healing from hurt, help me
to continue to be aware of where I am and continue
to grow to be the woman you called me to be.

Amen.

4

ENHANCING YOUR RELATIONSHIP WITH CHRIST

After I worked on my relationship with God and gave him all of me is when my life became better.

But you, man of God, flee from all this, and pursue righteousness, godliness, faith, love, endurance and gentleness.

—1 Timothy 6:11 NIV

L ife didn't improve for me until I made the conscious decision to surrender my life to Christ and be intentional about nurturing my relationship with Him. It required a commitment to live wholeheartedly for God. However, let's be clear, life's journey still presents its share of ups and downs. Embracing God doesn't exempt us from problems. But as we navigate through challenges and hardships, God's guidance becomes our steadfast support.

Enhancing your relationship with Christ requires effort, similar to nurturing relationships with friends or partners. Building this connection takes time and intentionality. For me, it began by inviting God into my heart and seeking forgiveness for my sins. I openly acknowledged and confessed everything I needed His forgiveness for, including sex before marriage and reliance on substances like alcohol to cope with pain. I was determined to make positive changes in my life, seeking God's strength to embrace celibacy and live according to His will. My desire was to fully believe again, to serve and love God wholeheartedly. My ultimate goal is to live in a way that pleases Him. I want God to look down at me and say, "Job well done."

A personal relationship with God is similar to the relationships you have with everyone else in your life. It's built on fellowship, love, and trust that exists between you and God. The Bible beautifully expresses this sentiment: "For God so loved the world that he gave his one and only Son, that whoever believes in him shall not perish but have eternal life" (John 3:16, NIV). It's truly awe-inspiring to think about God's amazing love and grace.

To pursue means to follow someone or something. My pursuit of enhancing my relationship with Christ required intentionality in how I lived my life and how I spent my time with God. The journey began with separating myself from sin, which was challenging initially. Yet, in moments when thoughts threatened to lead me astray, I found solace in the reminder of God's boundless love for me. The knowledge that God sacrificed his only Son out of love strengthens my resolve to avoid anything that might hinder my relationship with Him

I must admit that when I attended church as a child, I felt that having a relationship with God would be challenging. The church made it sound fancy and, at times, overwhelming. However, I later realized that building a relationship with God is quite simple—just by loving Him, relying on Him, praying, and communicating with

Him. When I made the decision to leave Chicago, I moved to Baton Rouge, and I truly believe that it was God's plan to lead me away from Chicago so that I could be in a place with fewer distractions and focus more on my relationship with Him. Now, it's just me and God, and I find solace in that connection.

That's when it all began. I found myself shedding tears, pouring my heart out to God. It was unbelievable how I had gone so long without allowing God to dwell inside me and walk with me daily. During that time, I embraced reflection, not dwelling in the past with regret, but genuinely contemplating my previous way of life. I earnestly sought forgiveness and offered heartfelt apologies. My desire was to establish a personal connection with God, to know Him for myself rather than relying on others' descriptions of His goodness. As a result, I developed a consistent prayer life characterized by authentic communication with God. No longer constrained by formal or "churchy" prayers, I spoke to Him with complete honesty, sharing my deepest thoughts and emotions:

Father God, in the name of Jesus, I love you. I need you. I do not want to live my life without you. I am lonely. I am struggling in the area of loneliness. Please keep my heart, guard my heart, and protect my heart, Father. It's broken. I'm lonely, I'm sad, and I'm not happy.

Being lonely used to be a significant hurdle for me. At one point, I found myself staying in a relationship primarily because I feared facing loneliness. However, I recognized that I needed to learn how to be comfortable with solitude and use that time to strengthen my relationship with God. Understanding God became intertwined with understanding my own identity and my place in Christ. So, during the periods when I intentionally spent time alone with God, I made a conscious effort to shift my focus away from my loneliness. Instead, I began to explore my passions and interests, discovering the activities that brought me joy and fulfilment. This solitude also provided me with the opportunity to gain a deeper understanding of myself as a woman. I came to realize that in the hustle and bustle of daily life and just living, I often neglected self-reflection and personal growth. But by dedicating time to living purposefully, I opened myself up to new perspectives and allowed myself to flourish.

When I say I focused on living, I mean specifically that I was merely going along with the motions—waking up, going to work, indulging in heavy drinking, partying, and engaging in gossip. During that time, I lacked any short-term or long-term goals, as well as dreams or aspirations. Essentially, I was just coasting through life without a clear direction. However, deep inside, I yearned for a more purposeful existence—one where I could strive to be my best self every day, with God right beside me. I realized that living my best life necessitated having God walk alongside me, guiding and supporting me on my journey.

When I relocated to Louisiana, my strong determination was to find a church that I could call home. For me, establishing a connection with a church was essential to fostering a meaningful relationship with God. Despite my efforts, I couldn't find a church that truly resonated with me. However, this didn't deter me from seeking a bond with God and spending time in worship. As a result, I found solace in worshiping at home.

Throughout my prayer time, I asked God to bless me with the presence of God-fearing women. My hope was to find companions on this spiritual journey, so I wouldn't have to navigate it alone. I firmly believe that having supportive partners makes life's challenges easier to bear. As the saying goes, "Birds of a feather flock together," indicating the power of surrounding oneself with like-minded individuals. Life is undoubtedly enriched when shared with others who share similar values and beliefs.

Prayer works, and it has rekindled a beautiful connection with a friend I've known since I was five years old. Together, we navigate life following God's path. In areas where I may be weak, she offers strength, encouragement, and holds me accountable. What was once a friendship has now evolved into a sisterly bond, and she is precisely the person I need to continue growing into the woman God intended me to be.

True growth does not solely arise from always being the strongest or smartest one in the room. It is imperative to surround yourself with individuals who challenge you, those who possess greater abilities and knowledge from whom you can learn. My friend, now turned sisters, happens to be one of those people. As I continue my journey with Christ, I am filled with confidence that God will provide for all my needs and grant me the necessary strength and wisdom.

Your relationship with Christ is an ongoing journey; it's a continuous and unceasing process. It's not about simply picking up God when it's convenient, but rather, carrying Him with you wherever you go. Personally, I prioritize my prayer life and consult God about everything. I make sure not to make any decisions without seeking guidance from Him. By maintaining a strong connection with God, you can hear His voice clearly as He communicates with you. And if you haven't heard from Him yet, hold tight; He's coming.

As I mentioned earlier, I used to live in Chicago before making the life-changing decision to move to Louisiana. Prior to the move, I deeply contemplated my actions and sought spiritual solace by inviting God into my heart, seeking forgiveness for my sins. Soon after, an intriguing opportunity emerged: I received a call about a promotion in Louisiana. Initially, I viewed it simply as a chance for professional growth, without immediately interpreting it as a sign from God. Nevertheless, I remained steadfast in my faith and continued to seek divine guidance, yearning for certainty that this move aligned with God's plan for me. My ultimate desire is to wholeheartedly follow God's path, acknowledging that building a relationship with Him involves laying a sturdy foundation of trust and unwavering faith.

Spending time with God is a deeply organic experience for me. Throughout the years, I have developed a profound love and connection with Him. If I were faced with the choice between the world and my devotion to God, I would unhesitatingly choose God repeatedly.

When seeking a relationship with God, it should come naturally and be something you genuinely desire. I remember waking up in the mornings and instinctively making time to talk to God and read the Word, whether it was through a Bible study or while worshiping to one of my favorite worship songs. For some, though, there's a tendency to turn this time with God into a rigid project. For instance, setting specific hours like 6 p.m. to 8 p.m. for prayer and reading the Word every day might sound dull or obligatory, as it did to me when I was a growing Christian.

Instead, I took a different approach. I integrated prayer into my daily routine: giving thanks to God while showering, worshiping and thanking Him as I drove home, and studying scriptures whenever I felt drawn to a particular book in the Bible. What made it even more exciting was the availability of Bible apps, which allowed me to explore and search for specific topics that aligned with my focus points for the day, week, or month. This flexible and organic way of connecting with God made the experience much more meaningful and fulfilling.

Following are some examples of how my prayer life started:

Prayer of Thanksgiving

> Father God, in the name of Jesus, I thank you for this day. I thank you for loving me. I thank you for saving me. I thank you for keeping me. I thank you for trusting me. God, you did not have to bless me with opportunities, but you did. God, you did not have to bless my finances, but you did. There is nothing I could ever do to repay you, Father, but I thank you. I love you. I trust you. I appreciate you!

Prayers Asking for Covering

> Father God, in the name of Jesus, I pray for my family. I pray for my mother, oh God, as it pertains to her health. No weapon formed against us shall prosper. God, you are a healer. You're a provider. You're the King of Kings and Lord of Lords. If my mother does not heal the way I want her to heal, I still love you, God. I still trust you, God, as you know what's best.

> Father God, in the name of Jesus, I come before you on my sister's behalf. Heal her heart, God. Growing

up, my sister struggled as it pertained to our mommy and having our mother actively in our lives. I know she's hurting, God. You know what we need, God. You know what she needs, oh God. Cover her. Heal her. Show her you're her provider; you're her doctor, her father, her mother. You are God. Without you, we are nothing.

Praying for Forgiveness and the Strength to Forgive Others

Father God, please heal me from lingering hurt and not being able to find it in my heart to forgive. I want to forgive others despite how they may treat me. I do not want to be forgiving and choosing to stay broken, which will get in the way of what you have for me. Father God, in the name of Jesus, keep me lifted; keep me encouraged. Even though they may have hurt me, I pray, God, that you bless them. God, I pray that you present yourself to them as you presented yourself to me, which allowed me to grow and flourish through you. God, I pray you comfort and guide them.

Praying for Forgiveness

God, I keep messing up. I want you, and I need you, but I keep messing up. I do know that you are a God that allows us to choose, you give us free will. Build me up, God, so I can be strong in you. Build me up, God, so when distractions come my way, I choose you because I know that it will lead to peace, grace, and favor. Choosing you will lead to eternal life. When I mess up, God, please grant me the grace and serenity I need to turn back to you and ask for forgiveness again. Thank you for loving me and giving me the chance and opportunity to grow in you.

These are the simple prayers I consistently offered as I cultivated a profound relationship with God. Let me tell you, God truly delivered on every one of those prayers for me. My mom's health is intact, and she's flourishing; her well-being is restored. Likewise, my sister's journey towards personal growth is remarkable; she's committed to becoming a better version of herself each day.

I can attest that when you pray, God attentively listens, and when you pray, God earnestly answers. Over the past few years, I've resided in various places, facing numerous challenges along the way. However, I consciously chose to lean on God and invest time in understanding Him because I knew that my ultimate help emanated from Him, and it will always continue to do so.

Professionally, I have encountered some challenging circumstances. During my time in Baton Rouge, Louisiana, I was responsible for managing the most demanding store within the company. This statement is not merely figurative; it is backed by statistics reflecting the location and demographics that contributed to its inherent difficulties. In order to navigate these challenging circumstances, I relied on my faith, seeking guidance from God through daily conversations with Him. His presence and support were instrumental in helping me navigate through those trying situations. Without His guidance, I would not have been able to overcome the obstacles I faced.

Working in Baton Rouge was a challenging experience; it felt like a constant struggle. Being all alone there, without anyone to lean on, was difficult. However, I came to believe that it was God's plan for me to be in solitude, as it allowed me to focus on my spiritual growth. Those tough circumstances actually brought me closer to God, and I found myself in situations where only His intervention could save me. It seemed as though God wanted me all to Himself, and that time alone enabled me to communicate with Him regularly. Simply talking to God every day became an essential practice that deepened my relationship with Him. Christ encourages us to have open conversations with God about anything and everything.

During times when I felt unsupported or my team seemed disengaged, I turned to prayer, asking God to instill trust in my leadership and for them to submit to my authority. Despite my earnest prayers, my desired outcome was not realized. Unfortunately, no one—absolutely no one—seemed willing to submit to my authority.

If I had not devoted time to establishing a relationship with God, I firmly believe that I would have mentally fallen apart. Living in Baton Rouge, I faced severe threats to my life due to the lack of structure and authority among the people there. It's hard to believe, but they would draw on the walls and leave handwritten notes with terrifying messages like, "Candace, I'm going to kill you," along with a specific date for their sinister plan. The situation was beyond unsettling.

In the face of these challenges, my father took immediate action and flew in on the first, expensive, last-minute flight to show his unwavering support and presence. "Who's messing with my daughter?" he demanded, demonstrating his protective love.

Despite the perilous circumstances, I remained resolute and determined. As a relatively young person in my thirties leading a tough team, I knew that my strength alone wouldn't suffice. Instead, I drew immense strength from my unwavering faith in Christ, firmly believing that I could overcome any obstacles that came my way..

Through these trials, my faith in God provided me with the resilience and courage to face each day. I held on to the belief that with God's guidance, I could navigate through the darkest moments and emerge stronger. Overcoming such adversities was undoubtedly challenging, but my unwavering trust in God's protection and guidance ultimately helped me persevere and find a sense of peace amid the turmoil.

The fire inside me burned fearlessly. Being the girl from the South Side of Chicago, I had never been intimidated by the craziness around me. I stood up fearlessly for everyone I loved and cared about, unafraid of the threats that life hurled my way. However, this particular situation demanded serious attention, particularly because the ominous message was repeatedly scribbled on the stall wall.

After seeking counsel, I approached upper leadership with my concerns, and their suggestion was for me to consider a permanent transfer to another city. However, deep down, I knew that I didn't want anyone to force me out of something I had worked so hard to achieve.

But then, something remarkable happened. Through grace and favor, one of the company VPs approached me with a unique opportunity. They invited me to work on a confidential six-month project at headquarters, alongside the executive vice president (EVP) of the corporation. Embracing the opportunity with enthusiasm, I accepted the offer, packed my bags, and embarked on this new adventure. It felt like God had intervened and lifted me up, protecting and guiding me even when I was hesitant to change my circumstances. In the end, God's plan surpassed all my expectations. Working for a Fortune 50 company alongside the EVP was beyond anything I could have imagined.

This experience reaffirmed my belief in the kind of God we serve—a God who cares for us, protects us, and wants what's best for us. My desire to live in alignment with God's will and be ready for whatever He has to offer became even stronger. I frequently found myself praying and seeking God and he consistently directed my path.

Praying for Guidance

> Father God, in the name of Jesus, I thank you for this day. Father God, I ask that you guide me so that I can always be in the position you want me to be in. I do not want to block my blessings, God. I do not want to get in the way of what it is that you have for me. Right now I am in a tough situation. God, no one is listening to me or trusting my leadership. Father God, guide me. Give me the words to say. Give me the strength to be the leader you need me to be to lead your people. If there is anything in me, God, that should not be, I pray that you remove it so that I can lead my team effectively. I pray that when I speak, they hear you, God. I pray when they see me, they see you, God. God, right now my work is chaotic; no one is listening to me or submitting to my authority. God, create an atmosphere of obedience. I pray they trust my leadership as it is effective because I am allowing you to lead through me because you live in me.

Talk to God about everything; that is the essence of building a strong relationship with our Father. Surrendering everything to God is essential - our lives, careers, families, as well as our minds and bodies. Trust becomes the cornerstone as we establish and nurture our connection with Him.

Don't pick and
choose what
to give to God.
Trust God with
all things, and
watch him move
on your behalf.

God, you can have all of me—not some parts but all. God, I want to be filled with your love, guidance, and Holy Spirit every day. Help me to trust that you have every inch of my life covered. You can handle it; you are God. Help me to trust that with you all is well. Choosing you, God, will help me to free myself of my fears while knowing you're taking care of all my needs.

Amen.

5

FINDING PURPOSE AND TAPPING INTO IT

My desires shifted when God gave me purpose.

For it is God who works in you to will and to act in order to fulfill his good purpose.

—Philippians 2:13 NIV

Many struggle with the concept of "purpose," and I must admit, I was intimidated by it as well. When I turned my life over to God, I often found myself specifically asking during my prayer time for help in discovering my purpose. I felt lost, unsure of where to begin. The idea of discerning God's plan for me was overwhelming—how could I even recognize His guidance? The word "purpose" seemed to trigger anxiety and a sense of incompleteness within me. While I was living my life fully devoted to God, I couldn't grasp how to live it with a clear sense of purpose. I delved into books and devotions about living a purpose-driven life, hoping to find answers, but still, I struggled to understand what that truly meant for my own journey.

Instead of stressing myself out, I made a conscious decision to prioritize my relationship with God. I became dedicated to seeking Him and deepening my connection with Him. My hunger and intentionality in pursuing this relationship grew significantly. Although I didn't have a church home in my current city, I refused to let that stop me from attending services. Despite the hours of driving it required, I consistently made the effort to be in the house of the Lord and worship with like-minded individuals.

After some time, I felt the need to revamp my morning routine to incorporate God in a more intentional manner. Like many people, I used to kickstart my day with up-tempo music, not necessarily Christian, but more along the lines of R&B – and truth be told, I still enjoy it, but I realized it needed a time and place. I yearned for something more inspiring while preparing for work, so I decided to listen to motivational messages or sermons instead. With that in mind, I invested in an iPad solely dedicated to my bathroom to listen to inspirational sermons while I got ready for work; no web browsing or social media distractions, just a tool for worship and spiritual growth.

To create a conducive environment, I adorned my bathroom with comfy stools, charming drawers, and bookshelves, all geared towards focusing on God and inviting His presence into my home. This designated space became a sanctuary where I could dress up, style my hair, and sip coffee while communing with God. In an unexpected way, this space became a channel through which God spoke to me about my life and purpose.

If you were to look for me, you'd likely find me in my bathroom, lounging in a cozy robe, listening to prophetic worship songs on my iPad, and immersed in prayer. This simple but purposeful change has brought a sense of peace and spiritual fulfilment to my mornings.

While some people acknowledged my diligent work ethic in my professional life, they had limited insight into my personal life outside of work. Many were aware of my strong religious beliefs, often asking questions like, "Which church do you attend?" or "What activities do you enjoy outside of work?" Fellow Christians were particularly interested in my beliefs, often inquiring, "Candace, what do you believe is your purpose?" When I admitted that I hadn't yet discovered any specific hobbies or a defined purpose, some would react with surprise, saying, "You don't know your life's purpose?" They would then offer various methods to help me find my purpose, without fully considering the significance of seeking guidance from God and allowing Him to reveal it to me in due time.

Recalling those conversations still makes me cringe. However, it's essential to understand that not knowing everything, lacking a concrete plan, or feeling uncertain about hobbies and life's purpose is perfectly okay and completely normal. The crucial thing is to give your best effort every day and walk with God on your journey. To create an inviting atmosphere for God and me, I invested in an iPad and adorable stools for my bathroom, along with other decor, creating a space dedicated to God and myself. It was a genuine effort, a way of trying, and actively putting my best foot forward each day.

"It was a moment that lifted away all my worries about my purpose, as I felt God's presence speaking to me." The memory is etched in my mind as if it happened only yesterday. I stood in my bathroom, engrossed in one of my favorite bishop's sermons, when suddenly, a gentle whisper filled the air, and I recognized it as God's voice.

"Candace, you are destined to lead." "Lead by example, and empower other women to strive for greatness."

After reflecting on my spiritual journey and realizing how far I had come, it became clear to me that the challenges I faced weren't just for my own growth but also to inspire others. I wanted people to see that they could experience true freedom by embracing God in their lives.

The revelation of a fragment of my purpose was like a breath of fresh air, filling me with renewed enthusiasm. This led me to seek God's guidance and ask for clarity regarding my path. Throughout my life, I had been blessed and admired not merely for superficial reasons but because of my compassionate heart and how I made others feel. People appreciated my work ethic and consistency.

Despite these favourable qualities, I struggled to comprehend God's specific calling for me. Each day passed without a clear answer. I diligently prayed and continued to live a life that reflected God's presence in me. My desire was for others to witness how their lives could be transformed positively by surrendering to God.

I felt a calling to lead, to be an example, and to empower women, revealing their true identities through their connection with God. My mission was to show them the potential they held within themselves and the strength they could draw from their faith.

As time went on, I remained persistent in my faith and commitment to be a living testament to God's love and grace. I yearned for others to witness the profound changes that could occur when they surrendered their lives to a higher purpose.

My journey has taught me that I am not only meant to find personal liberation through God but also to guide and inspire others toward their own spiritual freedom. With unwavering devotion, I will continue to live a life that reflects God's light, in the hope that others will be drawn to find their path to a meaningful and fulfilling existence.

When you wholeheartedly devote yourself to God, He reciprocates by speaking to you and guiding you. This journey requires unwavering commitment. As I continued to show up without relying solely on my own understanding, God's messages kept flowing in. It was during one of these divine moments that I heard Him say, "Start a mentorship program." At first, the idea seemed improbable. Me? Launching a women's mentorship program? Nevertheless, as I reflected on the countless women who had been inspired by my determination over the years, it began to make sense.

So many individuals had approached me with inquiries like, "How did you achieve your success?" "What motivates you to keep going?" "How did you get started on this path?" The demand for guidance was evident, and God had positioned me precisely where He wanted me: with a heart that was pure, honest, and receptive to His guidance. I realized that this was my calling—to lead by example and to provide tangible evidence for women to follow and find their own paths.

Hearing God's voice is not a singular event; rather, it requires patience and a true commitment to seeking His guidance, often involving fasting and sacrifices. When I first heard God's call for a "Women's mentorship program," I didn't have all the answers, and seeking His direction was an ongoing process to understand how to structure and implement it. As days turned into weeks and months, I dedicated myself to prayer and worship, desiring to stay attuned to God's voice.

Recognizing God's desire for me to embark on a mentorship program, I took action to bring this vision to life. Investing in a laptop and software to facilitate my God-given creation, I poured significant financial resources into realizing my purpose and utilizing my gifts. Throughout the journey of crafting the mentorship program, designing its sessions and courses, God revealed a profound message: "Candace, the sessions and courses you've created are the chapters of the book I want you to write."

The realization that my mentorship program was intricately connected to a book brought me a newfound sense of purpose and direction. It emphasized that following God's voice often leads to unexpected and intertwined paths, each contributing to His divine plan. With this revelation, I felt compelled to pursue the book alongside the mentorship program, knowing that both were integral parts of my calling.

I was in awe of what God presented to me. Everything became clear regarding his purpose for me to help lead God's people to Christ. While I am neither an author nor an English major, if it's what God wants me to do, it's what I'll pursue. I am going to write.

God spoke to me, revealing my purpose and even giving me the name for my business—A BETTER YOU—reflecting the belief that there is always room for improvement in every aspect of life. Initially, I couldn't secure an LLC with that name alone. However, knowing that God gave me that name, I turned to prayer and consulted a close friend. Then, my sister came up with the word "Experience." Thus, A Better You Experience was born, set to become the title of my series of books, beginning with Volume 1: A Better You Experience. It was a divine inspiration.

As God guided me, I realized my mission was to guide young women through a transformative journey, helping them become their best selves with God by embracing their roles as true Christian women and empowering them to be strong leaders, entrepreneurs, authors, and mentors.

I then began to see the grander purpose. God's intention for us extends beyond serving Him in a singular way. As beings created in His image, we are meant to reflect His multifaceted nature. Just like Jesus, who embodied various roles such as a carpenter, father, healer, and leader, we too can embrace diverse aspects of ourselves.

So, let go of the notion that God only has one specific plan for you. Life consists of different seasons, where God may call you to focus on one thing at a time and then shift your focus in the next phase. The ultimate aim is to align yourself with God's will, being exactly where He wants you to be. When you find that place, God will guide and communicate with you.

For me personally, I realized that there was more to my life than being the best boss or the hardest worker. I was at a point where God had something greater in store for me.

I remember one Christmastime like it was yesterday. My sister and I were at my parents' home in Ohio, eagerly opening our gifts. Inside, my father had thoughtfully included a beautiful note in each of our cards, expressing what he admired most about us. As my sister read her card, her face lit up with joy, listening to all the wonderful things our dad appreciated about her. However, when I opened my card, my heart sank a little. It merely said, "You're such a hard worker. Merry Christmas." That was all.

In that moment, it struck me that I needed to discover and embrace my true purpose. I realized that my identity goes beyond just my job. My calling is to serve God and His kingdom, no matter my profession or title. Whether I'm a doctor, lawyer, teacher, financial broker, or even a Fortune 100 company boss, it's all insignificant unless it aligns with serving God's purpose.

You are more than the degrees you hold or the job you do. Each one of us has a unique calling and a mission to serve others. Embracing this purpose is a personal choice, and we must take the initiative to tap into it.

When God places something in your heart, don't overlook the timing. Acting upon your purpose is vital; it requires building upon the foundation that God has laid out for you. It demands time, patience, and faith. For instance, I knew in my heart that I was meant to start a women's mentorship program, a calling that God had bestowed upon me and even provided the title, "A Better You Experience, Volume 1." At the end of 2019, He placed the idea of writing a book in my heart, and I knew I had to bring this vision to life. A great analogy is that God gives us trees, but we have to build the desk. Similarly, God showed me what to do and how to do it, but it was up to me to take action and get it done. "Remember, following your purpose is a journey, not a quick fix. It requires dedication and determination, but the fulfilment and impact it brings are immeasurable.

After recently relocating to another state and embarking on a new journey as a store director, my days became filled with long hours and intense work. However, within six months, my dedication and hard work paid off, leading to a well-deserved promotion to oversee one of the busiest stores in our group. It was an incredible achievement, and I approached each day with unwavering determination, always ready to bridge any gaps that arose.

Amidst the demands of my busy schedule, I also decided to pursue my purpose: writing a book. Despite the workload never seeming to lighten, I made a conscious effort to carve out time for my writing. Admittedly, consistency was a struggle initially—not because I doubted God's calling to write a book, but because I often felt mentally and physically drained. There were months when my laptop remained untouched, and my writing came to a complete halt.

Nonetheless, I persevered. I reminded myself of the importance of fulfilling my purpose alongside my professional achievements. I began implementing small changes to my routine, finding snippets of time during lunch breaks or early mornings to nurture my writing. As time passed, I discovered that even the tiniest increments of progress contributed to my overall sense of fulfilment. There were moments when I could only manage to type two sentences before bed, yet I still felt accomplished. I learned that something is always better than nothing.

While the journey hasn't been easy, I've learned valuable lessons about time management, self-discipline, and the power of passion. I've come to realize that pursuing one's dreams often involves pushing through the obstacles and finding ways to adapt to life's challenges. My determination to complete this book has become a testament to my resilience and a source of inspiration for those around me.

Though there are still moments of struggle, I now approach them with renewed optimism and faith in myself. As I continue to juggle the demands of my role as a store director and my passion for writing, I remain committed to seeing this project through to its completion. With each word written, I feel a deeper connection to my purpose, and I'm grateful for the opportunities that this challenging journey has brought into my life.

Work had become incredibly tough, draining me both physically and emotionally. I struggled, which led me to pray fervently every night, seeking God's intervention to lighten my workload and allow me to focus on my purpose and project. My commitment to spending time with God yielded regular moments of divine guidance. God

Candace Williams

reassured me that if my workload decreased, it would bring some comfort. At that point, I had achieved a certain level of success, and I knew that if I abandoned writing a book and starting a women's mentorship program, I would still be financially secure. However, the true motivation behind writing the book was to touch and transform souls. I sensed that writing the book was a crucial first step towards the next chapter of my life.

Despite my long and exhausting days, I found myself coming home and neglecting my project. Instead, I would pray and often break down in tears due to my weariness. The mental strength I once had to pursue my career passionately had waned. But one night, amidst my thoughts and prayers, I distinctly heard God's voice urging me, "Candace, I need you to fight for this like your life depends on it." And it was true; I genuinely felt that my life did depend on it. If I truly desired to change my circumstances, I knew I had to push forward with unwavering determination. Regardless of how exhausted I felt or how much it hurt, I had to persevere. Writing my book and working on my mentorship program were not just options; they were essential for my growth and fulfilment.

The weight of responsibility hung heavily over me. I knew that it was something I had to undertake. Failing to act would mean missing out on my season and the opportunity to bring to life something I believed God had bestowed upon me. I could no longer allow years to pass without taking action; procrastination was no longer an option. Despite feeling exhausted, I could no longer use fatigue as an excuse, for I knew I had to fight for God, just as He had fought for me on the cross.

Although my days were long and draining, there were also sleepless nights. Yet, none of my efforts were in vain because, in the end, God's glory will shine through when women read my book. They will find encouragement and inspiration, connecting with God in ways they never experienced before.

After a long day at work, I found the need to motivate myself and establish a connection with God. Just as I made space for God in my life, I also needed to create a designated writing space, a place where God's inspiration could flow through me and my thoughts could take form. Despite having a beautiful office with exquisite furniture at home, I rarely used it for its intended purpose. Instead, I'd lounge in my comfortable swivel chair, indulging in naps and relaxation on my days off. The TV became an idle companion, and I found it challenging to concentrate on any one task for an extended period. Consequently, the idea of sitting in my office to write seemed overwhelming. However, I took steps to make my workspace more conducive to creativity and tranquillity. I added a cute fireplace and played prophetic worship music to calm my mind and create the perfect ambiance for God's messages to flow through my writing.

Discovering one's purpose demands dedication and a willingness to embrace it fully. It is essential to tap into that purpose and let God work through us. Allowing our purpose to lie dormant within us is not an option; instead, we must strive to live intentionally, embracing God's guidance in our lives. Personally, I am determined to nurture my purpose and avoid letting it wither away. By setting an example, I hope to inspire others to recognize that they, too, can become better versions of themselves by allowing God to lead their paths.

The beauty of purpose
is that you know exactly
what you should be doing
and how. This means you
no longer have a taste
for anything outside
of your purpose. Get
to your destiny, sis!

Father God, I want to be used as a vessel here on earth. If there is anything inside me that's not like you, God, please remove it. I want to be used as a vessel in the earthly realm. God, show me purpose. Show me what it is you want me to do, so I can serve you and live a life that is according to your will. I don't want to live life randomly but with true intention every day.

Amen.

6

TIRED OF MAKING THE SAME MISTAKES

Kept growing and did not look back.

As a dog returns to its vomit, so fools repeat their
folly.

—Proverbs 26:11 NIV

Yes, it was me standing at the altar every Sunday, seeking
forgiveness from God for my actions - sleeping with my
boyfriend, smoking weed, and using foul language. I
continuously put myself in situations where I knew I would have to
repent. Strangely, I began to find solace in my brokenness, embracing
the pain and hurt that came with it. Isolation became my refuge,
avoiding interactions with others. I'd rather stay home, drown my
sorrows in a bottle of wine, cocoon myself in a blanket, and hope that
sleep would numb the pain. I sought validation and opinions from
people around me, rather than focusing on what God truly wanted
for me. Tearfully, I would repent and beg God for forgiveness, only to
find myself back in the same cycle within a couple of weeks. Exhausted
and emotionally drained, I felt burned out and overwhelmed.

I truly believe that God gives us all opportunities for transformation and growth. The question we must ask ourselves is, are we tired of making the same mistakes? Are we at a point in life where we're prepared for God to work through us, allowing Him to guide us towards success rather than being in a position of struggle? For me, that moment of readiness came before my breakup. As I've shared earlier in this book, I vividly remember sitting in my car, in the parking lot of my job, completely exhausted. I had grown weary of building relationships without a solid foundation, and living a life not aligned with God's will. I had been attempting to navigate life on my own, without involving God in my decisions. It was at this point in time that I finally embraced the idea of partnering with God, seeking to follow His path and teachings. I became eager to try things His way for a change, ready to live a life in harmony with His purpose.

How many of us can relate to making mistakes? I certainly have made my fair share of them. I've gone out of my way and found myself in deep holes of sorrow. We all have weaknesses, those things that hinder us from reaching our destinies. For me, it was a particular man who kept me from becoming the woman I knew I was meant to be. I've mentioned him briefly before - we were in an on-and-off relationship for about ten years, and it led me down a deep path.

When I was ready to get my first apartment, I needed a co-signer and some furniture. I turned to my dad, and he came through for me, co-signing and helping me order a sofa and dining set. However, I made a mistake by not being completely honest with him. I didn't mention that I intended to move my boyfriend in with me. I wanted my dad to help me secure an apartment and furniture for both of us. It was foolish of me to do so, as I was moving a man into a place my parent had helped me get. Although my boyfriend contributed to the rent and utilities, it was still a misguided decision to keep it from my parents. Instead of focusing on becoming a better version of myself, I was too preoccupied with proving my love and worth to him. Looking back, I should have appreciated the beautiful apartment my dad secured for me and prioritized personal growth, rather than sneaking my boyfriend in.

If my boyfriend were the man God called for me, I believe he would have embraced God's way and taken the necessary steps to show his commitment. Unfortunately, that wasn't the case, and our relationship took a different path. We ended up living together for almost two years before eventually breaking up. After a year, I was fortunate to be promoted to a new position, and we decided to move together once again. This time, he took the responsibility of getting the townhome and utilities in his name, but we continued to live together.

During this second phase, everything began to fall into place, and I started to see his true character. As I mentioned before, he wasn't faithful and was involved with multiple women behind my back. Realizing this, I made a swift decision to pack up my belongings, including furniture, TVs, and decor, and moved out. He was left with his clothes and a small TV.

This experience has been challenging, but it has also been a valuable lesson for me. I've learned the importance of staying true to my values and not compromising on what I know is right for me. Though it's painful, I trust that God has a better plan for my life, and I am hopeful for a future where I will find someone who truly cherishes and respects me.

You would think that the last time I put myself in an awful situation would be the end of it. Yet, years had passed, and I found myself in the same predicament—falling in love and moving in with another man. All I craved was to be loved and have someone to look forward to every day. The fear of being alone pushed me into these hasty decisions, but I had reached a breaking point and realized I needed to do things God's way. It was time to break the cycle of making the same mistakes.

Upon reflection, I understood that men were not the root issue; rather, my lack of wise decisions was the problem. My personal life began to affect my profession, leading to countless errors because I wasn't thinking clearly and living without God's guidance. This unhealthy pattern persisted for years and eventually led to a mistake that landed me in my boss' office.

I had grown tired—both mentally and physically—of living without God's direction. So, I made a conscious decision to change my ways. Staying focused wasn't easy; it required pushing myself to make a genuine difference. I knew it wouldn't be as simple as snapping my fingers and hoping for improvement. It demanded effort and determination to break free from the old habits, which I did by going cold turkey.

Now, my focus is on aligning my life with God's plan, making thoughtful choices, and living with purpose. It's an ongoing journey, but one that brings me peace and fulfilment, and I am determined to stay committed to it.

God was the sole reason behind the blessings of a job offer and the opportunity to relocate to another state. This significant shift allowed me to make immediate changes in both my social circle and lifestyle. While I could have easily maintained the status quo, and remained as the same old Candace, I made a conscious decision to embrace change. I meticulously outlined the transformations I desired in my life and set clear goals for myself. Every day, I dedicated myself to hard work and self-improvement, fuelled by the desire to learn from past mistakes and not repeat them. Through prayer, I sought guidance and strength to overcome my failures and to pursue positive changes with unwavering determination.

Obviously, making mistakes isn't limited to just issues with sex, drugs, and alcohol; it can manifest in various aspects of life. During my upbringing, I possessed a stubborn streak, and I was resistant to anyone's advice. Coming from a middle class family, my actions were often perceived as those of a spoiled, affluent individual, as described by my cousin.

As I entered my twenties, I had a thing for driving fast - pushing speeds over a hundred miles an hour, to be precise. Regrettably, this reckless behavior led to a terrible driving record, including getting pulled over twice in a single day, with only five hours separating the incidents. Despite these close calls, I persisted in speeding and accumulating more traffic violations, which eventually resulted in multiple arrests and the need for bail. During these distressing situations, my cousins and younger brother would come to my aid, acting like responsible older siblings by bailing me out. Unfortunately, this process involved paying a significant amount of money; I remember having to shell out at least $4,000 multiple times. Looking back, I'm grateful that I managed to get the bail money back after fulfilling community service requirements. However, it's evident that my actions were incredibly irresponsible, and I deeply regret putting myself and others in harm's way.

There was a pivotal moment in my life when I believe God presented me with an opportunity to make a better choice and change my ways. It occurred during the last time I got pulled over for speeding, which, truth be told, was not a surprising offense for me. However, my dismay grew when the officers informed me that not one but two arrest warrants had been issued against me. They promptly arrested me, handcuffed me, and took me to jail. As we headed to the police station, my mind raced trying to comprehend how I had ended up with two warrants. Eventually, I discovered that it was because I had failed to show up in court for previous citations. My negligence in attending court was a result of my busy work schedule, which prevented me from prioritizing my legal responsibilities.

The situation worsened as I learned that my bail was set at $50,000. Desperate to secure my release, I needed to come up with $5,000, which I simply didn't have. In my moment of distress, I reached out to my ever-supportive aunt, the one who had consistently been there for me throughout my life

They organized the women inmates in one line and the men in another. On that day, I had taken the time to doll myself up, getting my hair done before heading to work. As I stood there, I couldn't help but notice the male inmates whispering amongst themselves, their eyes fixed on me. "Look at her," they murmured, directing their comments solely at me, among the hundred other women in line. Their curiosity got the better of one guy, who finally blurted out loud enough for me to hear, "What'd they get you for?" His bewilderment was evident, as if my appearance didn't fit the typical mold of someone in this situation. Reflecting on that moment, I couldn't help but see my own foolishness. This wasn't my first, second, third, or even fourth arrest, yet I failed to learn my lesson.

As I waited in a cell at the courthouse, my heart raced with anxiety, anticipating my meeting with the judge and the possibility of being bailed out. If the bail wasn't paid within the next thirty minutes, they were going to take me to Cook County jail. The other women in the cell gathered their belongings, getting ready for the bus that would soon transport us all to Cook County. Panic began to set in, but the other women urged me to remain calm. They questioned my decision to spend money on bail when I could simply endure a three-day jail stay and be free until my next court appearance. However, I couldn't fathom going to jail. I explained that I was waiting for my aunt to bail me out because I wanted to avoid that experience altogether. A girl shouted, "Girl, that's a waste of money. Just go to jail. It's only three days, and the staff there are nice." I observed that these women seemed to be accustomed to such situations, having it all figured out, with seemingly nothing to lose. However, that wasn't an option for me. I had a thriving career and responsibilities as the head of a work center with people depending on me. The thought of going to jail was something I wanted to avoid, so I made the choice to pay my bail.

As they urgently yelled, "Fifteen minutes. The bus is arriving," to the inmates, their voices suddenly changed direction, calling out my name, "Candace, you can now see the judge to post bail." With that, they approached the cell, swung it open, and led me on the path to meet the judge. Walking down the hall towards the courtroom, a heart warming sight greeted me – my aunt and cousin, clutching five thousand dollars in cash. Their unwavering support was evident; my cousin's face beamed with the purest joy, knowing she was rescuing her beloved cousin, while my aunt's expression held a tinge of disappointment, perhaps grappling with mixed emotions.

With bail secured, my freedom was temporary, contingent upon my fulfilment of 250 hours of community service. In the ensuing months, I dedicated myself to this task, striving to make amends and give back to society. After being let go on bail, I was required to fulfill 250 hours of community service. Over the course of several months, I diligently completed my community service obligations, and finally, the day arrived when I regained my freedom.

God grants us all a way out. When I received my chance, I embraced the opportunity and ran with it. I grew weary of constantly making mistakes and finding myself back at the same crossroads a week later. It was crucial for me to shift my mindset, and that required a complete transformation of myself.

Making mistakes can act as barriers to realizing one's true destiny. Personally, not having my mom's support in the way I needed left me feeling low, with minimal guidance and encouragement when I faced obstacles. Consequently, I had to navigate through challenges on my own. However, this should not be an excuse to ignore responsibilities or avoid necessary actions due to a lack of support or guidance. Even though pursuing self-improvement can be daunting when you're going solo, having someone by your side can ease the journey. Feeling tired of regressing, I developed a strong passion for progressing towards my goals.

I know I have mentioned numerous times that I did not have anyone to help build me up. That was because there were not any examples that simply showed their downfalls through vulnerability and honesty. I needed someone to walk me through what they did to overcome their mistakes. Many women told me what I should be doing and what I should not be doing. They told me I was going to hell because the life I was living was not of God. I needed more. I needed something tangible to help and guide me. But not having that did not stop me from tapping into God heavily. It took a lot of self-discipline because I was walking this path on my own. I was tired of making mistakes. I wanted a fresh start. And I wanted to be brand-new. God did just that for me. I went cold turkey and refrained from many of the old things I used to do. I tapped into learning and putting my best foot forward every day.

Mistakes are an inherent part of this process, and they offer opportunities for growth and transformation. Through recognizing and learning from these missteps, you can pave the way for positive life changes and align yourself with your calling.. Remember, it's the willingness to evolve and improve that truly defines your path to becoming the best version of yourself.

I wanted to evolve into a more effective and inspirational leader. Gone were the days when I sought to control others to serve my interests and boost my image. Though I had always possessed an impressive work ethic and a determined spirit, I knew it was time to shift my mindset and leadership approach. My goal was to use my position as a platform to set a tangible example and motivate my team to achieve their aspirations. I aimed to empower women to realize that they could achieve greatness through hard work, without relying on anyone else for validation or success.

Embracing this new vision for leadership, I committed myself to personal growth and self-awareness. Every day, I tirelessly worked on improving my leadership skills. I took a closer look at how I communicated, ensuring that my words were empowering and supportive. Upholding a strong sense of integrity, I maintained a professional demeanor and adopted the mindset of "This is who I am."

The results were remarkable. As I changed, I could see an immediate positive shift in my team dynamics. I gained their trust and support as they felt inspired and uplifted. By embodying what they aspired to become, I earned their buy-in and dedication to our shared vision. My transformation not only impacted my life positively but also served as a shining example for others to witness the power of authentic and compassionate leadership.

God grants everyone an opportunity for an exit, a path to change. Moreover, He has bestowed upon us the gift of free will, enabling us to make our own choices. Now, the question arises: what choice will you embrace? Opt to take that exit, so you can fulfil the purpose of becoming the woman God has called you to be.

If you've always
done it your way
and always gotten it
wrong, why not give
God a try? He will
never let you down.

God, you can have me, all of me. I do not want to do things my way anymore. I have done things my way time and time again, and it has gotten me nowhere. I want to do things your way. I want to do things according to your Word, will, and purpose for my life. God, I have experienced your good works when I am obedient. Keep me aligned, and continue to give me the strength to trust so that I can always choose you.

Amen.

7

SELF-CONFIDENCE WHILE WALKING WITH GOD

*Comparison kills confidence, while positive
thinking increases confidence.*

Trust in the Lord with all your heart and lean not on
your own understanding; 6 In all your ways submit
to him, and he will make your paths straight.
—Proverbs 3:5–6 NIV

S elf-confidence is the essential belief in one's abilities, qualities,
and judgments. It signifies having trust in oneself, which is
crucial for personal growth and success. While I have faced
my fair share of challenges, self-confidence has seldom been a major
struggle for me. However, during my early childhood and adult years,
I encountered situations where others projected their insecurities onto
me, and regrettably, I allowed their negativity to affect me. As a child,
I faced ridicule and prejudice due to my dark skin, enduring hurtful
remarks and teasing on hot summer days when I dared to be outside.
It was disheartening to hear some parents making snarky comments
like, "Candace is too black to be outside in the hot summer sun. I can't

believe her parents allow it." These hurtful experiences had a profound impact on my self-esteem and made me question my worth.

One day, while playing in a friend's backyard, I overheard my friend's mom making hurtful comments about my skin color. She suggested that I should leave before her husband, who had issues with dark-skinned individuals, returned home. This experience stayed with me as I grew older, enduring teasing and hurtful remarks from others because of my dark skin. Even some of the girls I hung out with would make negative comments about my appearance, leaving me confused and hurt.

Despite the negativity around me, I managed to maintain a sense of self-assurance and found beauty when I looked in the mirror. One day, I shared my feelings with my mom, asking her to look at me and then at me again while looking in the mirror. I was trying to understand what others saw when they looked at me. My mom assured me that I looked exactly like the girl in the mirror, leaving me puzzled but determined to embrace my self-perceived beauty – I knew I was beautiful!

Over time, I came to a powerful realization: I am beautiful both inside and out. I learned to appreciate the confidence I had in myself and to disregard the hurtful opinions of others. Embracing my uniqueness became a source of strength, and I grew to admire the person I was becoming.

Now, I hold my head high, knowing that true beauty comes from within, and I'm grateful for the self-assurance I have gained on this journey. Though I faced challenges, they have made me resilient and appreciative of the beauty I see in myself.

An essential attribute of self-confidence is the ability to ignore what others think of you, and that resonates with my own experiences.

I have always been someone who didn't let others' opinions affect me, which allowed me to tap into my confidence from a young age. Not being overly concerned with what others thought about me empowered me to stay true to myself and pursue my passions without fear of judgment. This self-assurance has been a driving force behind my personal growth and achievements.

Walking hand in hand with God, I am anchored in faith throughout my entire adulthood. This journey has been a testament to my steadfast reliance on God's guidance, trusting that He will always pave the way for me. True confidence, for me, emerges from understanding and embracing all aspects of myself—the strengths and weaknesses—and taking ownership of them. This confidence, in turn, intertwines seamlessly with my faith walk with God.

I have grown into a woman who knows her inherent value and the unique contributions she brings to any situation. My motto, 'Actions speak louder than words,' serves as a guiding principle in my life. Embracing the identity of a woman of God requires profound self-assurance in the person God created me to be and the courage to walk confidently towards the promises He has bestowed upon me. Thankfully, this confidence has shielded me from the discouraging voices of others. If I lacked confidence, the voices of others would have deterred me from reaching my destiny.

Remaining true to yourself and staying focused on your path are crucial keys to personal growth and fulfilment. During my young-adult years, I was strong-minded and confident in my identity, yet I found myself yearning to be accepted by the cool crowd – seeking fun without accountability. However, this approach caused me to overlook the purpose and destiny that God had intended for me. I discovered that unlocking my confidence required moments of solitude, where

I could connect with God. While it meant missing some parties and events, the experience allowed me to explore uncharted aspects of myself.

Although the concept of "isolation" may conflict with our instinctual desires, I realized the significance of spending time alone, delving into my true identity as a woman, and liberating myself from external influences that tried to define me. The results were – my mind felt refreshed, my productivity at work soared, and I even received a promotion. I gained a deep understanding of my self-worth and developed a clear vision for my future. I began to take charge of my life, confidently pursuing new roles and negotiating salaries that aligned with my true value. Today, I stand tall, brimming with self-assurance, and grounded in the knowledge of who I am and what I want.

Throughout my journey, I realized that building my self-esteem required walking hand in hand with God. I made a conscious effort to uphold a high level of integrity in all my actions. One particular incident stands out in my memory when my boss scheduled a crucial meeting. He wanted to discuss the possibility of me taking on a challenging role in a different location, and he asked about my salary expectations. After years of working on my confidence, I mustered the courage to state a deserving figure, and to my delight, it was accepted. Now, I stride forward with boldness, embracing faith, and trusting God to guide me through life's endeavors.

Being confident in who you are requires choosing yourself and moving in a way that the opinions of others do not matter or affect you. I experienced this firsthand when I was promoted and took on the responsibility of running the busiest store in the company, located in Texas. It was a unique situation as no one else in the area looked like me for more than two hundred miles. Nevertheless, I embraced my confidence and had faith that I was exactly where I was meant to be, knowing that God had a plan for me.

During my time in Texas, I faced challenges related to racism and ageism, as I was not only a black individual but also in my thirties, leading a significant team. People would often question my position, asking incredulously, "You run this entire store?" or "What happened to the previous leader? I thought they were doing a great job!" The comments didn't offend me; instead, I took them as a form of flattery, realizing that I was breaking barriers and achieving something remarkable.

In reality, this was not my first leadership role. It was, in fact, the fourth store I was running, and I was also responsible for leading over 170 team members. Understanding the magnitude of my accomplishments, I felt immensely blessed. Being a woman, a person of color, and in my thirties, I was doing something seemingly impossible and unheard of. This realization fueled my determination even more, and I pushed myself and my team to do their best.

As a result, my team found an inspiring example in me—a trailblazer who showed them what was possible with hard work and determination. I embraced this role wholeheartedly, and together, we achieved great success, surpassing expectations and proving that anyone, regardless of their background, can make a significant impact with unwavering self-belief and dedication.

In Texas, on the day of the inventory check, an executive visited my location and started voicing concerns that were not directly related to inventory matters. While I tried to maintain transparency, he seemed intent on finding something to critique as my team had been well-prepared. Despite this, I remained humble and accepted his feedback. However, I couldn't help but wonder why he was focusing on other store concerns rather than the inventory itself.

As the day progressed, the numbers were finally announced, and to my amazement, we had outdone ourselves! Our efforts resulted in reducing shrinkage by more than a quarter of a million. We had achieved a record-breaking goal, and I couldn't contain my joy, immediately celebrating with high-fives for several team members. Finding a quiet corner, I offered prayers of thanksgiving, shouting in delight, "To God be the glory. My team did it!" It was an unprecedented achievement for that location, which had never experienced such a significant reduction in the past.

God's amazing grace has been evident throughout my life's journey. Despite facing discouragement from others, I chose not to be deterred from achieving my goals and instead embraced my truth with conviction. I firmly believe that God placed me in Texas for a purpose, and failure was never an option in my mind. With unwavering confidence and trust in God, I navigated through challenges, confident that everything would align according to His plan. My actions were guided by humility and faith, as I carried Christ with me, seeking His direction for my team and decision-making.

Admittedly, my unshakable confidence and deep faith in God might have seemed unconventional to some. However, I remained steadfast in who I am and continued to trust God, even in the face of threats to my life. I refused to back down or retreat, convinced that if it was God's will for me to be in that place, He would protect and guide me. Fear never dictated my actions; instead, I relied on the assurance that God's hand was leading my way.

My journey has taught me resilience, unwavering faith, and the power of trusting in God's divine plan. Embracing my truth and standing firm in my beliefs have led to extraordinary accomplishments and unwavering strength in the face of challenges. I have learned that with God by my side, there is no obstacle I cannot overcome.

God opened another opportunity, providing me with a chance to extricate myself from my current situation, not through ridicule or force but through divine guidance. Standing firm in my identity and the promises God had bestowed upon me, I embraced the chance to work with the EVP of the company, a door opened amidst all the chaos.

Confidence and trust in God placed me in a position of recognizing my true worth. Believing in my abilities, I knew I could take my talents anywhere and achieve success. This conviction also instilled in me the belief that I am not replaceable. Thus, after twenty years with a company, I made the bold decision to embark on a brand-new venture. My sole focus became listening to God's calling for me, particularly in becoming the woman He envisioned.

Feeling a definite sense of transition, I understood it was time for something new. My confidence in this being a God-ordained move for my life fueled my determination. I trusted in the words I heard from God and began seeking new roles in other companies. However, my search initially proved fruitless as no jobs matched my current salary level.

Yet, I did not lose faith. Instead, I decided to pause my search and continued giving my best effort in my current role. Each day, I showed up with determination and dedication, fully committed to making a difference.

Several months had passed when I received a phone call from a former colleague, telling me the company he worked for was looking for new leaders. I was extremely excited and overwhelmed with joy.

God was preparing me mentally for transition. I was looking for roles and even entertained interviews and salary discussions; God put it inside me. With obedience, I had begun looking. If I had not started looking at other places of employment several months before, I might not have been mentally prepared for what God had for me, which was to transition to a well-known *Fortune* 50 company. After twenty years, I was ready for change and for the destiny I knew God was preparing me for. After several interviews and months later, I was offered a position, which I accepted.

Accepting the position was not the end. It required me to make another move. Here I was, a young black girl born in Chicago, where I lived for over thirty years. My first move to Louisiana was preparing me for my second move to Texas. If I did not decide to leave Chicago, would I have decided to accept this new opportunity and move to Georgia? I was prepared to be stretched so I could grow. I trusted God confidently on my journey, and he prepared me.

Prior to interviewing for and accepting the role in Georgia, I had a conversation with my dad. He was worried about the transition. I was doing an amazing job in my current role and made a name for myself professionally. In his eyes, this career move came out of nowhere, and I was already secure. He was right. But playing it safe was not good enough for me. I knew my worth, and I also knew I would be an asset and flourish wherever I decided to take my skill set. My dad was in a panic. "Candace, why are you leaving? Is everything OK? You're doing so well there."

"Yes, Dad. Everything is OK. It's time for a change, and I will be OK."

Confidence has been ingrained in me since I was a young girl. It all began when other kids started commenting on my appearance.

Despite having big legs (or as some would say, big-boned) and dark skin, I knew I was beautiful.

As I grew older, I learned not to let others' opinions deter me. When the time came for me to move and purchase a home, someone questioned whether I would need to downsize, given that the home I had been renting was spacious and stunning. They assumed that I couldn't achieve something better or bigger. God has blessed me with a stunning, more spacious home in one of Georgia's most desirable communities. I immediately responded with a firm "no." Why should I downsize when I believed that God was leading me to something greater? I've always had confidence in my faith, trusting that God will fulfill the desires of my heart. It's essential to stay focused on God's promises rather than getting distracted by what others say.

Remember, you shouldn't be swayed by the opinions of others. Instead, keep your faith in God and trust the process. Walk with confidence as you know that God is guiding your path.

How can you truly become the woman God has called you to be without being secure and walking confidently in the promises he has set for you?

God, keep me confident in the woman you created me to be. Keep me confident in the woman you have called me to be. You created all of us in your image. God, help me to have the confidence and faith to know when things are not going as planned. All things are still working together for the good of those who love him.

Amen.

8

EXPLORE AND MAXIMIZE POSSIBILITIES IN YOUR LIFE

*I can't afford for God not to have his arms
around my life. I have to get to greater.*

Now to him who is able to do immeasurably more
than all we ask or imagine, according to his power
that is at work within us.

—Ephesians 3:20 NIV

All things are indeed possible, and I am forever grateful for the transformative journey that God has taken me on. Often, we tend to look at our current circumstances and use them as excuses for why we cannot progress in life. We allow our perception of reality to convince us that we won't achieve greatness or improve. However, this is far from the truth. It's essential to recognize that you can surpass limitations and embrace the abundance of possibilities that God has in store for your life. The key lies in allowing God to live through you, so you can confidently walk in the promises He has made for you.

Despite growing up with both parents in the household, my life took an unexpected turn when my mom experienced a nervous breakdown and grappled with mental illness. I found myself lacking the traditional mother figure that others had. It wasn't because she didn't want to be there for me, but rather her mental illness prevented her from doing so. Witnessing my friends' mothers taking them to school, engaging in heart-to-heart talks about crushes, and going shopping together, I couldn't help but feel the absence of that maternal support. These are the experiences most young girls go through, and I yearned for that connection.

While facing suspensions and nearly repeating my sophomore year, I still managed to graduate from high school on time with my peers. I then attended a junior college for two years before embarking on the journey of applying to out-of-state universities. After submitting numerous applications, I received the news of my acceptance into a university, and I felt an overwhelming sense of pride and accomplishment. I had overcome several challenges throughout my life, including my struggles in high school, but I persevered and was determined to do better – starting with pursuing higher education away from home.

During a college open house, I couldn't help but notice that most of the girls had their moms accompanying them, while I was accompanied by my dad. It wasn't until after college that I came to realize the emotional burden I had been carrying all along, stemming from my mother's illness and her absence from our home. Nevertheless, I cherished the fact that I had made it this far, though my understanding of my journey was still evolving.

School was an incredible experience where I had the chance to live on my own in a dorm and meet new people. However, things took a turn for the worse one day when I found myself involved in a fight. As a result, I was suspended from college and had to return to Chicago. My suspension was a consequence of my inability to handle the challenges life threw at me. The situation arose when a friend of mine was being bullied, and I attempted to intervene and break up the fight. Instead of seeking help, I reacted impulsively when someone hit me, and the situation escalated, leading to my suspension. It was a devastating blow, especially considering the hard work I had put into getting into that university, with two years of schooling left.

A significant realization during this time was that in order to embrace the opportunities that God had in store for me, I needed to confront my fears and past hurts. Growing up, I had seen my mother unable to stand up for herself, which subconsciously influenced my behavior. I ended up taking on her unexpressed struggles, speaking up and defending myself when necessary. Unfortunately, this sometimes translated into a rebellious and unruly attitude, with me pushing back and speaking up in inappropriate settings.

However, this difficult phase allowed me to embark on a journey of healing and self-discovery. As I worked through my past hurts, I learned to redirect my focus and energy towards positive growth. It was during this healing process that I began to grasp the true extent of God's grace and favor in my life, which motivated me to strive for genuine improvement.

Now, I am determined to turn things around and make the most of the opportunities presented to me. I have come to understand the importance of responding thoughtfully and constructively to life's challenges, and I am committed to making better decisions moving forward. While my suspension might have derailed my college graduation plans temporarily, I believe that with perseverance and a newfound sense of purpose, I can still achieve my dreams and fulfill my potential.

Upon reflection, I returned home from college, and fortunately, my part-time job at the time enabled me to keep working even after finishing school. As a cashier earning approximately $6.15 per hour, I was unwavering in my determination to excel in my role and continually enhance my performance. Another pivotal moment in my life, highlighting my unwavering dedication to turning challenges into opportunities, occurred when I earned the trust of the restaurant owner. Remarkably, even at the tender age of fourteen, I was entrusted with the significant responsibility of closing the restaurant. I served as the pace setter and the sole individual with the keys to lock up.

As a cashier, I honed my skills and found ways to increase my scan percentage, becoming the go-to person for taking returns on the sales floor due to my speed and efficiency. My hard work and positive attitude caught the attention of someone who saw potential in me and offered me a supervisor position. Grateful for the opportunity, I reflected on my past experiences with supervisors, identifying what I admired and what I believed needed improvement. Armed with this knowledge, I embraced my new role and worked to bridge any existing gaps.

My can-do attitude impressed the store manager, and when we closed the store together in the evenings, he relied on me for support. I gladly assisted anyone who needed help, even if it went beyond my responsibilities as a cashier supervisor. It was clear that my dedication and willingness to take charge were recognized and appreciated by the team.

I feel fortunate to have turned my part-time job into a full-time opportunity and progressed from a cashier to a supervisor. My commitment to excellence and adaptability has allowed me to excel in my roles and positively impact those around me.

In less than a year, a new opportunity came knocking: an assistant manager position with a salary of $55,000. To my surprise, some of my college-educated friends were still earning less than that. In my twenties, I hadn't fully grasped the reality of my situation yet. As a young black woman from Chicago, many had written me off, especially considering my troubled past—fighting throughout high school and even getting suspended from college. But here I was, with my foot in the door, determined to make the most of this chance.

I approached the role with unwavering dedication, showing up every day and putting in the hard work. I didn't have a clear plan when I returned home from college, but I was committed to giving my best effort each day, and that seemed to open doors for me.

As the years passed, I grew into the position, becoming an assistant manager in various departments of the store. Looking back, I can't help but laugh at the journey I've been on. Some even called me a "beast," a term I took as a compliment because it showed how I dominated my role daily. I credit my success to allowing God to work through me, enabling me to reach heights I could never have imagined.

After gaining experience as an assistant in various areas of the store, the time came for the district leaders to select a comanager who would assist the store manager in its operations - a stepping stone toward applying for a store manager position. Given my outstanding performance as an assistant, I was eager to interview for the role. Unfortunately, my first interview did not yield the desired outcome, but I took the setback as an opportunity for growth and learning. Constructive feedback revealed that in addition to excelling in my duties, it was essential to demonstrate business acumen and effectively communicate during the interview process.

Undoubtedly, my leader had faith in my capabilities to fulfill the comanager role, but I needed to overcome the interview hurdle. During the interview, I encountered an embarrassing moment when one of the interviewers asked if I had prepared practice questions. The interview was conducted over the phone, allowing me to have notes as a reference, but I made the mistake of reading my answers verbatim. This rigid approach hindered the natural flow of the conversation. Reflecting on this experience, I recognized it as a valuable learning curve, especially since it was my first time interviewing in six years, and on top of that, it was for a high-level position.

Despite the initial setback, I remained determined to improve and prove my capabilities. Armed with the lessons learned, I embraced the challenge of demonstrating my skills and expertise more effectively in future interviews. With dedication and perseverance, I was confident that I could eventually secure the comanager role and continue progressing towards my goal of becoming a store manager.

I was truly grateful for the valuable feedback I received. Rather than letting it affect me negatively or giving up, I used it as motivation to work even harder. My dad played a pivotal role in this process by encouraging me and reminding me that I had the ability to answer those questions easily. He pointed out that my real-life experiences were more than enough to handle the interview successfully. His words resonated with me, and I made sure to keep them close, showing up every day with renewed determination. I understood that staying present in the moment was essential, and I trusted that another opportunity would arise.

After a few months, a new opportunity presented itself, and I seized the chance to interview again. Armed with my dad's feedback and my six years of experience in leadership, team-building, and problem-solving, I was well-prepared to answer their questions confidently. This time, I was promoted to a co-manager position, but I didn't stop there. Instead, I used the role to gain knowledge in other aspects of the business, areas I hadn't previously worked closely with. I delved into understanding P&L budgets and honed my skills in handling and elevating current leaders in the store, navigating through difficult conversations.

Had I given up when faced with rejection, I wouldn't have achieved the co-manager position, which was a significant step towards eventually running a multimillion-dollar store. As six more months passed, I found myself interviewing for a store manager position. It wasn't something I had meticulously planned; rather, it unfolded naturally. I believe that God's favor played a role in providing me with opportunities to grow within the company. Throughout this journey, I remained diligent, working hard every day, and giving my best effort in all that I did.

It was the morning of my interview, and I felt confident in my over seven years of leadership experience, during which I had demonstrated my ability to drive business growth and boost sales rapidly. Despite acing the interview, I was ultimately not selected for the position, and I couldn't help but feel disappointed. The disappointment aside, I couldn't deny the dedication I had shown during the four months I filled in as the store manager when my current manager was on leave. Running the store like my own, I achieved exceptional results.

Throughout the process, I reminded myself of the belief that whatever was meant for me, no one could take away. I knew I was well-prepared and trusted that God would bless me with the right opportunity in due time.

Several months later, when another store position opened up, I was asked to interview again. This time, I felt even more prepared and confident. I seized the opportunity and aced the interview, leading to the incredible news of being selected as the store manager for a substantial $70 million store in a Chicago suburb. It was a moment of triumph that made me reflect on my journey.

Coming from humble beginnings as a young black woman from Chicago, I had faced challenges and had often felt like an outcast. However, through hard work and perseverance, I broke barriers and became the store director with responsibility for 150 team members and six managers. It was crucial for me to remember where I came from to keep myself grounded.

In reaching this milestone, I recognized the importance of leveraging the gifts and talents God had instilled in me. I embraced hard work and ensured that I not only succeeded but also supported, taught, and trained my team effectively. It was never just about me; I wanted to inspire and demonstrate what was possible for others.

I refused to let my past define me or limit my potential for the future. Instead, I created my path to success and allowed myself to flourish. Looking back, I realized that every step of the journey, even the disappointments, had led me to where I was meant to be.

Exploring and maximizing the possibilities in your life requires taking action: to explore, to maximize, and to pursue your goals. Everything good in this world is intended for us by God. Why wouldn't you want God's best for your life? Despite facing a suspension due to a poor decision to fight, I didn't let it deter me. Instead, I focused on personal growth and eventually attained the highest position at my store as the store director. We can achieve our goals if we have the determination to do so—the choice is in our hands. Let's not give up, as God is with us every step of the way.

When I look at my sister, who grew up in the same household without the presence of a mother figure, I see her determination to be the best version of herself daily. Despite the challenges, she's become a successful teacher and a great mother, driven by her desire for God's best in her life. God's supernatural power can comfort and support us if we allow Him to walk with us through life's journey.

Misery loves company," as the saying goes. It reminds us that being mindful of the company we keep is crucial if we strive to be our best selves. To move in the right direction and realize our full potential, it's essential to surround ourselves with like-minded individuals who share our mental space.

Advancing to the next level is nearly impossible if we choose to spend time with people who lack the desire to grow. While working at a Fortune 100 company, I had the opportunity to collaborate with a team member who was actively striving for a promotion to the role of supervisor. This individual serves as an excellent illustration of dedication and ambition within our team. Despite having all the necessary credentials, he recognized the need to improve his business acumen. While already intelligent, educated, and familiar with the business dynamics, he understood the significance of refining his appearance and communication skills. During our conversation, he surprised me by stating, "Candace, I won't be hanging out with some of my friends this week. I'm focused on enhancing my professional communication and elevating myself." His maturity in acknowledging the changes he needed to make was commendable. He genuinely wants to better himself and comprehends the steps required to reach his goals.

God desires prosperity for each individual, and the world is filled with abundant resources, both external and within ourselves. This message is conveyed not necessarily through spoken words but through a deeper, spiritual connection. A young man aspires to unlock the full potential of his life, striving to become a better version of himself, a sentiment often overlooked by many. Often, we get trapped in the belief that we are set in our ways, refusing to change how we speak, dress, or act. Consequently, opportunities pass us by because we resist growth and improvement. It's essential to recognize that when an opportunity is presented to us, someone sees potential in us, and it might be an invitation to elevate ourselves to become better.

We must remember that not everyone will comprehend our journey, and it's not their duty to do so. Our path is personal and sacred, a connection between ourselves and God. To fulfill God's purpose for our lives, we must keep our minds focused on His will and diligently work towards it. For instance, I was divinely inspired in the summer of 2019 to write a book. The message was clear and direct from God, and I felt an unshakable urge to fulfill this mission. Even amidst my career transition into a new company, I proceeded with outlining and titling the book, determining its core content. However, at some point, I hesitated and stopped writing.

In 2020, I decided to pick up the book again and started writing little by little. I was determined not to give up on it, even if I could only find time to write sporadically. However, in the spring of 2021, I found myself talking to a friend about my struggle to find time to focus on the book. I realized that completing this book was the key to launching my women's mentorship program, which was a dream and a calling I felt deeply about.

I expressed my exhaustion to my friend, admitting that my demanding career felt like it was constantly standing in the way of my destiny and purpose - writing the book and starting the mentorship program. Nonetheless, I held onto the belief that the challenges and obstacles I faced were not mere coincidences but part of God's plan. I knew that my experiences were meant to be a blessing for other women, helping them avoid the countless mistakes I had made along the way.

Realizing the need to make adjustments in my life, I acknowledged that my heavy workload left me with little energy when I returned home. Consequently, I came to the conclusion that I had to prioritize and possibly limit some of my extracurricular activities to create more space and energy for my writing and the mentorship program.

During a conversation about extracurricular activities, someone shared an invaluable piece of advice with me: "Every day, do something. Write, even if it's just a page, a paragraph, or a sentence. Take five minutes to make progress." Additionally, she emphasized the importance of listening to God's voice and knowing when to rest. Taking this wisdom to heart, I diligently followed these principles until I felt God urging me to take my project, my book, to the next level. Despite my friends' invitations to hang out, unwind, and travel, I knew I couldn't afford to follow their lead. There was a higher calling I had to answer, and becoming a best-selling author meant I needed to fully dedicate myself to the task God had entrusted me with years ago. It wasn't that I had anything against enjoying life or spending time with friends; my focus was simply on fulfilling God's plan. Politely declining their invitations, I stayed true to my purpose, working diligently and maintaining a clear and focused mind, attuned to God's voice. While some gossip and misunderstanding surfaced, alleging that I was acting differently, I chose not to let it bother me. My priority was to complete what God had called me to do, and with unwavering determination, I pressed on.

Persistence is key; there's no room for discouragement. Stay focused and trust the process, for success often demands sacrifices. Don't find yourself merely observing others' achievements from the sidelines; take charge and move forward. Success lies within our grasp, and it's up to us to seize it. Avoid limiting yourself and embrace the opportunities God has in store for you. Allow Him to work through you so you can fully realize your potential and purpose. Explore and maximize the unique individual God has called you to be.

You owe it to yourself to not only be the best version of yourself. You owe to others as well! We need you! We are watching! Keep paving the way for us!

God, I want to be absolutely everything that you called me to be, and not just so I can be my very best self but for others as well. Others need to see me healthy and whole. Others need to see how amazing life can be if we keep you first. As a Christian woman, I deserve the absolute best, and that is what you want from me. You did not call me to live a mediocre life. Keep my eyes on you, God, so I can reach my full potential and continue to become and evolve.

Amen.

9

OUTLINING GOALS THAT ALIGN WITH YOUR PURPOSE(S)

Stay aligned with the will of God.

He has shown you, O mortal, what is good. And
what does the Lord require of you? To act justly and
to love mercy and to walk humbly with your God.
—Micah 6:8 NIV

A beloved prophet, who holds a special place in my heart,
once stated that there are only two ways to do things: God's
way or God's way. And she couldn't have been more right.
There is no alternative to following God's path. Prior to embracing
this message, I took some time to come to this realization. As I
climbed the leadership ladder, I believed I had my life perfectly
planned out. However, I soon realized that my ambitions were not
in harmony with God's will. As I grew closer to God and integrated
Him into my daily life, I recognized the necessity of making Him a
part of every aspect, including my career. This revelation came to me

during the summer of 2018 when I was uncertain about my purpose and calling. At that time, my focus was solely on work and performing well, without considering God's plans for my life.

As I remained steadfast in my focus on God and committed to doing my best, my life's purpose gradually unfolded before me. It became my responsibility to align the goals I had set for myself with the calling I received from God. That calling was clear—to lead, encourage, and inspire women to reach their full potential. In a previous chapter, I shared how God communicated with me, guiding me to launch a women's mentorship program, write a book, acquire property, and pursue various endeavors in the marketplace.

To deepen my connection with God and gain further clarity, I dedicated more time to living a life fully devoted to Him. Through this devotion, I received precise instructions on how to begin my journey, prompting me to revise and realign my goals to harmonize with my true purpose.

Goals and purpose should align; ideally, they should be one and the same. In my journey, I came to realize that there was only one path: God's way. I took a closer look at my aspirations and what God intended for me. As God instilled a sense of direction within me, I carefully mapped out my calling. It's essential to reach a point in life where you're not merely living in the present moment but have clear goals and a well-defined plan for your future, even if you haven't discovered your ultimate purpose yet. Trust the process, seek God's guidance, and lead a devoted life committed to God, and eventually, your purpose will reveal itself.

Now I had a clear purpose that I fully understood on a professional level. My primary goal was to empower others and help them reach the next level of their careers. This involved guiding supervisors towards executive roles and assisting executives in becoming store directors.

My motto became, "No man, no woman left behind," signifying my commitment to encouraging and supporting individuals in their pursuit of growth.

Part of my calling and purpose is to inspire people to envision a better version of themselves and provide the necessary push to achieve it. Witnessing individuals experience personal and professional growth is deeply gratifying to me. As a leader, I felt responsible for helping those who were eager to progress and attain higher positions within the organization.

Furthermore, I aimed to positively impact the lives of those who might not have seen a brighter future for themselves, but I aspired to encourage them every day. Seeing their spirits lifted and confidence boosted was incredibly rewarding. Aligning this goal with my purpose brought a sense of fulfillment and meaning to my work.

I actively engaged with each member of my team, holding one-on-one meetings to ensure their success. I set the stage for their growth and development, providing support and guidance wherever needed.

Apart from my career-focused objectives, I also set out to achieve a personal ambition – writing a book. To make this dream a reality, I established a deadline and a feasible timeline. By breaking down the process into daily writing objectives, I could work steadily towards completing my book. I remained committed and held myself accountable throughout the journey

Simultaneously, I pursued personal goals, like writing a book, by staying disciplined and focused on meeting self-imposed targets. This sense of purpose and drive gave profound meaning to both my professional and personal endeavors.

One of my primary goals was to establish and launch a women's mentorship program. To achieve this, I carefully defined its structure, created a roadmap, and dedicated myself to its realization every day. I felt a strong calling to lead and set an example, which meant being open and honest about my own life experiences - something I believe mentors and influencers should do more often. With my vision in mind, I also designed my website and templates while sharing the challenges I faced in life and how I overcame them, all of which I'm eager to share on my website. All my goals are in harmony with my purpose and calling.

Throughout this journey, I learned that it's alright to reassess and reinvent yourself. While I had grand plans for my life, my daily interactions with God made me realize that the vision I had for myself might not necessarily align with His vision for me. Consequently, I took the necessary steps to realign my priorities with my purpose.

God has promised to bless me with my dream home and car, but I understand that it requires proactive effort on my part. I firmly believe that faith without action is ineffective, so I am diligently working towards my dream home, which holds a value of over $1 million. In pursuit of this vision, I am leveraging all the gifts that God has bestowed upon me, aligning myself with my destined path.

While keeping God's promise in mind, I am also ensuring that my financial affairs are in order. I have made sure to stay current on my taxes, maintain timely bill payments, and clear off all debts, ensuring that I don't find myself in an uncomfortable financial situation. The same principles apply to attaining my dream car.

It's essential to note that both of these dreams are not just materialistic pursuits. They are reflections of the qualities that God has instilled within me, shaping my desired lifestyle and allowing me to give back to others in meaningful ways.

By combining faith, hard work, and responsible financial management, I am confident that I am on the right path to realizing these dreams, all the while acknowledging that the journey itself is a testament to God's guidance in my life.

God promises that if we keep our minds focused on Him, He will grant us the desires of our hearts. I hold onto this belief for my life, aspiring to attain the best, including wealth for my family, and I have faith that God would guide me towards it. However, I am always mindful that loving money itself is sinful, as mentioned in Timothy 6:10 (NIV), "For the love of money is a root of all sorts of evil." Nevertheless, I knew that being wealthy as a Christian isn't inherently wrong, as long as we use our riches to bless others and glorify God.

To achieve financial prosperity, I realized that I needed to put in the hard work and act upon God's guidance. I envision myself as a successful multimillionaire, and to make that a reality, I must take concrete steps towards it. My plans include investments in real estate, as well as opening a coffee bar and women's spa, all of which have the potential to bring in wealth. I carefully mapped out a strategy that aligned with my goals and purpose.

I have my goals outlined and understood that they wouldn't just materialize on their own. It required diligent effort and perseverance. I created a goal board, similar to a vision board, during a recent Christmas. On this board, I laid out six short-term goals. While some of them have already come to fruition, I continue to have faith in God for the remaining ones.

My pursuit of wealth is based on the belief that God would lead and bless my endeavors. I acknowledged the responsibility to use any wealth I gain to positively impact others and give glory to God. I diligently worked towards my goals, knowing that action, aligned with my purpose, is essential in achieving success. With unwavering faith, I remain hopeful that God would continue to guide me towards fulfilling the desires of my heart.

One significant achievement that came to fruition was my pursuit of travel and the strengthening of family traditions. Though seemingly simple, both goals hold immense value for me. I'm often described as traditional, and my passion for family extends not only to immediate members but also to aunts, uncles, and cousins. In the past two years, I have genuinely connected with many cousins whom I previously had little interaction with. To achieve this, I took deliberate steps to shape our family traditions. Upon relocating to Atlanta, I ensured I had a spacious home, capable of accommodating not just my immediate family but also cousins, uncles, and aunts who may visit. During holidays, I eagerly invited my family to join me, resulting in frequent out-of-town guests every three months. It was no accident; I actively pursued these connections. My desire to be more involved with family and preserve traditions drove me to make these intentional efforts.

In my life's purpose, I aspire to lead, encourage, and motivate women to improve themselves. A crucial aspect of personal growth is healing, which I discovered involves delving into the depths of one's identity and understanding why we are the way we are. This journey to self-awareness is significantly aided by learning more about our family history. Instead of waiting for family reunions, I sought to foster relationships with family members and create meaningful moments of connection. During challenging times, I have found immense comfort and reassurance from my family, second only to my faith in God. I recognize that everyone has their unique perspective on family, shaped by individual circumstances, and that is perfectly acceptable. However, for me, preserving and cherishing family traditions hold great importance.

Every time I look up, I receive a call from family members who want to visit and spend time together, and it brings a smile to my face. It feels like a testament to the fact that God truly answers prayers. I had asked for a spacious home where everyone could stay comfortably, and God has graciously granted that wish.

At times, you might find yourself unsure of your purpose, even though you have a clear set of goals. During those moments, I encourage you to fearlessly move forward and pursue the vision God placed in your heart. Seek out God's guidance through prayer, and allow Him to lead you along the right path. Pray that God reveals your purpose to you.

Prayer

God, I am here seeking your face and your voice. I want to live a life that is aligned with your will for me. I want to do what you want me to do. God, I no longer want to do things my way. Walk with me, God. Show me what you want me to do here on the earth. Use me as a vessel, Lord, so you can do what you need to do for your people in your kingdom. Use me, Lord. Guide me. Right now I have plans for my life, and I want to be confident that this is what you want me to do. Speak to me. I'm listening. Amen.

Before God revealed His purpose and calling for my life, I was focused on setting and achieving my own goals, primarily short-term ones. Like many other women I've encountered, my aspirations were centered around having a husband, a successful career, and a few children. I had meticulously planned everything, including my career in Baton Rouge, Louisiana, the new city and state to which I had relocated.

However, despite having achieved professional success and embracing a new life, I found myself still longing for a partner, a husband to share my journey with. I was single and unhappy, and many nights were spent in heartfelt conversations with God. I implored Him, reminding Him of His promise to grant the desires of my heart if I delighted in Him. I had uprooted my life from Chicago for a fresh start, hoping to minimize distractions and deepen my focus on God. Yet, I couldn't help but wonder, "Where is he, God? Where is my God-fearing, handsome, and financially secure husband?"

As I prayed and sought answers, God began to reveal His divine plan for me. He showed me that there was a greater purpose beyond my initial desires. Instead of merely seeking a husband, I needed to embrace the journey of self-discovery and spiritual growth. He reminded me that true fulfillment lies in aligning my will with His, not just seeking my own wishes.

Over time, I learned to trust in God's timing and surrendered my desires to His divine wisdom. As I wholeheartedly sought Him, He opened doors I never anticipated. He led me to opportunities and experiences that enriched my life, molding me into the person I needed to become. I realized that God's plan was far grander than what I had envisioned for myself.

Today, I understand that my calling is not just about finding a husband or achieving personal success. It's about living in alignment with God's purpose and using my gifts to make a positive impact on the world. Through God's grace, I've found contentment and joy in this journey, knowing that He holds the perfect plan for me, even if it deviates from my initial expectations.

Before God revealed His purpose and calling for my life, I had set personal goals and diligently worked towards each one, primarily focusing on short-term objectives. Like many women I've encountered, my aspirations included having a husband, a fulfilling career, and a few children. It was a well-laid plan, and I was living in Baton Rouge, a new state, and city, advancing in my career. However, I hadn't found a life partner, and this left me feeling unhappy and unfulfilled. Countless nights were spent in deep conversations with God, pouring out my heart, saying, "Lord, you promised to grant the desires of my heart if I delight in you. Here I am, having left Chicago for a fresh start, seeking to minimize distractions and focus on you. But where is he, God? Where is the God-fearing, kind, affluent husband you have in store for me?"

Oh my, there were numerous nights when I felt utterly disheartened. To be honest, "discouraged" doesn't quite capture the depth of my emotions. I found myself awake in the wee hours, shedding countless tears. I was in such distress that I reached out to my cousin, who had recently tied the knot. She is a truly compassionate and kind soul; she became my rock during that challenging period. Thankfully, her husband was away at the time. We would spend hours on the phone, from 9 p.m. to 5 a.m., with me pouring my heart out, lamenting, "Where is my husband? I feel so lonely. I don't want to be here all alone with no friends, no man."

She listened intently and reassured me that everything would be okay. With empathy in her voice, she opened up about the years she spent being single and going through moments of sadness. "You know, Candace," she began, "I've been there too. I experienced tough times and loneliness, but now I'm happily married. If I had to relive it all to end up where my husband and I are today, I wouldn't hesitate to do it again."

I stood strong and remained committed to being the woman I knew God intended me to be. I believed that God had called me to a season of singleness, a time to draw closer to Him and listen to His voice. Over time, I found solace in my single life, understanding that it's alright to shed tears, yet not dwell in sorrow indefinitely. I refused to lean on my cousin as a crutch any longer, embracing the new beginning God had granted me.

This transition wasn't about doom and gloom; rather, it marked a fresh chapter, guided by God's divine plan. I made a conscious choice to live according to God's will, even if it meant not having found a husband or having children yet. I knew in my heart that my life had purpose, and I trusted that God was orchestrating each step I took. It is written that the Lord orders the steps of the righteous.

God's guidance was the compass for navigating this world, and my task was to remain patient, seeking Him, and attuned to His voice (Psalm 119:13 NIV). Although I might not have had a clear purpose at first, I prayed fervently for God to reveal my calling and life's purpose. I held onto the assurance that God wouldn't leave me hanging; He would speak to my heart in His time.

Embracing the process, I allowed God to shape me and lift me up. Trusting in His plan, I eagerly anticipated the fulfillment of His promises – the arrival of my husband and children were yet to come. Until then, I resolved to continue living a life devoted to God's guidance and will.

Start working on the goals you set for yourself. During my time in Baton Rouge, where I was independent and alone, I remained focused on God and the promises I knew He had for me. Immersed in my career, I honed my leadership skills, striving to be more effective for my team. Setting professional objectives, I consciously refused to be complacent and instead embraced continuous reinvention. While awaiting divine guidance, I dedicated myself to these goals.

It was undoubtedly a journey—a balancing act of working, returning home, spending quiet moments with God, and venturing out for solo dinners. However, God's presence never left me for long. Miraculously, within less than a year, a promising opportunity arose, and I seized it with determination. Throughout this waiting period, my prayer to God was to avoid complacency and instead persistently improve myself.

When I eventually moved to Texas, God's voice resounded crystal clear, revealing His purpose for me.

When purpose emerges, everything you once cherished becomes unfamiliar. Previous passions lose their appeal, as if your palate has undergone a profound change. Take this as an encouragement for your journey towards greater things. Embrace the discomfort, as it serves to bring you closer to your destiny. Remember the saying, "Rome was not built in a day." Stay patient and open to hearing from God; it takes time. In my own experience, it took a few years after fully dedicating my life to God, not just dipping one foot in the door and retreating. God will eventually unveil your purpose, aligning your goals with it.

The only thing that is getting in the way of success is you. Pray, make a plan, execute, and work hard at it every day. Don't let up, sis!

God, as I am outlining goals for my life, I pray
that they are aligned with what you want me to
do. And I pray that my goals align with who you
called me to be. Help me not to make decisions
based on what I want to do. Help me not to get
distracted by my wants and desires. Keep my
mind and eyes on what your desires are for me.

Amen.

10

IMPROVE YOUR EFFECTIVENESS BY STAYING FOCUSED

Starve all distractions.

Brothers and sisters, I do not consider myself yet to have taken hold of it. But one thing I do: Forgetting what is behind and straining toward what is ahead,
—Philippians 3:13 NIV

I discovered my true potential when I learned to minimize distractions, let go of my past, and wholeheartedly focus on my future. I know many of you have experienced moments where staying both focused and motivated seemed challenging. For me, during times when concentration is crucial, I direct my attention towards my current mission and future aspirations, finding guidance in my faith in God.

Previously, I went through a phase in life where everything seemed to be going wrong, both personally and professionally. However, things took a positive turn when I regained my focus.

Sometimes, to make progress, one must decline invitations to dinner parties, movies, or casual hangouts with friends – activities we would otherwise engage in regularly.

I vividly recall a day at work when I performed terribly due to being consumed by thoughts of the person I was dating at the time, making it nearly impossible to concentrate. To be clear, there's nothing wrong with dating or having crushes. The problem arises when these relationships become distractions, hindering our personal growth.

In such situations, it's essential to ask ourselves, "Why am I allowing this situation to impede my progress and potential for greatness?" By recognizing and eliminating distractions, I have learned to stay focused and committed to my goals, ultimately leading to positive changes and achievements in my life.

The distractions I faced were profound and detrimental. The person I was involved with exhibited cheating, narcissistic behavior, and verbal abuse, which led to physical altercations between us. As a result, I found myself discombobulated, unable to function or think clearly. Despite showing up for work daily, my performance suffered, leading to poor decisions and ultimately, termination from my career. It was a consequence of allowing the chaos in my personal life to interfere with my professional world. While the company did eventually rehire me after several months, I now realize that it could have been entirely avoided had I chosen to live my life in alignment with God's principles. Living a life guided by faith would have kept my mind clear and enabled me to make sound decisions.

Once I made positive changes in my lifestyle, my professional career took a turn for the better. Embracing a God-fearing life allowed me to regain focus and unknowingly tapped into my creativity because my thoughts were clear. This transformation involved addressing the aspects of my life that were hindering my relationship with Christ, such as embracing celibacy, practicing kindness towards others, sharing and giving, building a strong relationship with Christ, and dedicating myself to it daily.

Looking at where I stand professionally today, I can see the remarkable progress I've made. Embracing a God-fearing life has brought me to where I am now, and my salary has multiplied by almost five times. I am grateful for the positive changes that have taken place and credit them to living a life centered on faith and devotion to God.

The turnaround for me was the day I pulled into the parking lot of my job and told God I only wanted to do what he wanted me to do and live the way he wanted me to live. If I did not choose the life that I am living, which is to choose God, I would not be in a good place—not from a financial standpoint, but mentally, it would have been bad. I chose to get focused and dial into what God had in store for me. My future and getting there are important to me.

You just can't wake up one day and decide you want to make six figures or be a multimillionaire without actively working on it. Getting there requires being focused so you can be effective and get results. After being with a company for almost twenty years, I transitioned into a new company. I was in a toxic relationship, living my life the way I wanted, not in God's way. There is no way I would have been able to learn, grow, and be promoted after only being with the company for almost nine months in one of the busiest stores in our group. I have spent the past several years training my mind and creating boundaries for myself. In return, I am always able to prepare so opportunities cannot pass me by. I train my mind to control my emotions and to be able to think for myself and not be negatively influenced by others. I set boundaries by giving myself timelines, not being easily accessible, not saying yes to everything, and not having to go everywhere all the time with everyone. I prepare myself by taking advantage of opportunities when they come my way and not settling for less.

As I embarked on this new journey with a different company and in an unfamiliar role, the transition proved to be surprisingly smooth, largely due to the years I had dedicated to staying focused. This preparedness allowed me to absorb everything like a sponge, and I finally found myself in a position where my progress was evident. I became effective and laser-focused, showcasing the positive outcomes of leading a God-fearing life, which was noticed by those who knew my background and origins. However, achieving this transformation required a complete overhaul in all aspects of my life.

While my skill set and experience were undoubtedly contributing factors to my success and facilitated the transition, I soon realized that they alone were not sufficient for this new professional setting. Consequently, I needed to reset my mindset and enhance my skills to not only lead at a higher level but also to familiarize myself with the company's unique processes and routines.

In my previous role at a different company, I was accustomed to merely getting things done efficiently. Still, in this new position, I discovered that success hinged on much more than just completing tasks. It involved elevating the entire team, which meant investing time and effort in developing, teaching, and training staff. In the past, I thrived on being a problem solver, akin to the TV character Olivia Pope, rapidly achieving results and moving on to the next challenge. That approach had served me well in my prior professional world, where promotions and challenging assignments were frequent.

However, in this new role, the focus shifted towards cultivating a cohesive team and fostering growth within the organization. I had to adapt my leadership style and embrace a more long-term perspective, emphasizing team development over quick fixes. This change presented a new and exciting challenge that required me to evolve as a leader and refine my approach to achieving results.

The transition into this new company and role was smooth due to my focus and preparation, but it also demanded a significant shift in mindset and leadership approach. By recognizing the importance of team development and growth, I embraced this fresh opportunity for personal and professional growth, and I am committed to making a lasting impact within the organization.

This experience was unlike any other. It wasn't solely about personal ambition and securing a promotion with a shiny bow on top. Instead, it required a different approach, one that involved tapping into the potential of my team and fostering their growth. To succeed in this new role, I realized the importance of truly understanding my team members and leaders on a deeper level. This involved taking the time to know their professional aspirations, goals, and strengths.

Contrary to the assumption that all leadership roles share the same desires, I discovered that many leaders in the corporate world focus solely on their own success, often pursuing immediate results without investing in their team's development. However, in my new position, the emphasis was on people development, which challenged me to cultivate skills I hadn't previously used.

To be effective in this role, I understood that my accountability extended beyond the workplace; it began in my personal life. How I spent my time outside of work mattered because I was responsible for others' growth. Consequently, I became more mindful of my choices during my downtime. To maintain focus, I adopted a routine that included having dinner and going to bed early for adequate rest. I found using a planner during my off-hours to be immensely helpful, enabling me to plan my days and weeks efficiently. Additionally, I leveraged the note app on my iPhone to stay organized, ensuring I accomplished every task on my list before the day's end, whether it was paying bills, scheduling appointments, or completing household chores. Though seemingly straightforward, staying organized was pivotal in becoming effective and achieving meaningful results.

In my new position, my focus and dedication allowed me to quickly close gaps and achieve success. Every day, I approached my responsibilities with a clear understanding that I held the well-being of others in my hands. My mindset underwent a transformation, shifting from solely pursuing personal results and accomplishments to helping others thrive professionally and reach their better selves.

Remaining focused both inside and outside of work is a key factor in my effectiveness as a leader. I lead an honest and consistent life, striving to practice what I preach. Integrity, humility, and respect for others are crucial qualities for being an effective leader. My aspiration is to be a woman whose presence reflects godliness, inspiring others to want similar growth, not out of envy, but because they genuinely recognize the positive influence of my actions and the presence of God working through me. I aim to be a source of inspiration, helping others discover their true potential with God by their side.

Ascending to the top can be a solitary journey, as not many can accompany you on that path. Embracing this natural loneliness while relying on a spiritual connection with God is essential. Maintaining emotional composure and minimizing distractions are keys to maintaining effectiveness in this journey.

Once you achieve success, the question arises: who will you extend your help to? Whom will you encourage, motivate, and empower? Many believe that the challenges we face in life are meant to teach us valuable lessons and facilitate personal growth, which holds some truth. However, my aspiration is not solely to excel individually or to be the most accomplished, but to witness others thriving at their best. To achieve this, I must become a genuine example for others, openly sharing my own trials, roadblocks, successes, and failures.

Effectiveness should extend beyond the confines of the workplace; it should permeate all aspects of life. I constantly remind myself that I want to be the kind of woman my nieces look up to and strive to emulate. I hope that one day they will surpass my accomplishments, and I aim to be a source of inspiration for my nephews as well. I desire that they seek qualities in the women they date that align with those they see in their aunt.

As I continue to tap into the woman God created and called me to be, my motivations have shifted from personal gain to becoming a blessing to others. My ultimate goal is for others to witness the presence of God within me. It's important to acknowledge that we cannot save everyone, which is a painful reality I had to come to terms with. However, we can have a profound impact on those who genuinely seek help and improvement. Even for those who are resistant to change, our existence serves as a representation of the potential they too can achieve in life.

Achieving success should not be an isolated journey; rather, it should be a stepping stone to uplift and support others. By becoming a positive role model and assisting those who are willing to be helped, we can make a meaningful difference in their lives and, in turn, inspire them to be their best selves.

I am the eldest child in my family, and I believe that to some extent, my siblings' current positions in life are influenced by my actions and choices, whether they acknowledge it or not. They can see my success and witness the significant role God plays in my life. Being focused and effective has been important to me, but now I have a more profound purpose: to lead by example, motivate, and empower others to follow a similar path - not merely by words but through my actions.

My sister has always been distinct, unafraid to take risks and challenge the status quo while staying true to herself. As we grew up in a Christian household, our family had a strong religious influence with my dad playing the drums at church, and my grandfather serving as the pastor. After his passing, my uncle took on the pastoral role. Although there were God-fearing women around us, they didn't seem relatable or accessible. It was as if we were living in separate worlds, lacking young women to look up to, mirror, and seek encouragement and guidance from.

I desired to become that tangible example for my sister - a God-fearing young woman who follows the right path. I aimed to be someone who not only talked the talk but walked the walk. I didn't want to be someone who encouraged others to be better while living a double-minded life myself.

So now, my mission is clear - to continue being successful and devoted to God while serving as an inspiration to those around me. I want to be the woman my siblings can look up to, trust, and find encouragement in as they navigate their own journeys in life. By consistently living my values and staying true to my principles, I hope to make a positive impact on their lives and the lives of others.

Not too long ago, my sister told me that I am a role model for her. This revelation brought everything full circle, affirming the reasons why I choose to live my life the way I do. Unlike simply going with the flow, my sister actively works on bettering herself and creating a lasting legacy for her children. She observes my life choices, whether it's moving to a different state, seizing new job opportunities, pursuing promotions, or diligently working on improving my credit and building savings.

On the other hand, my brother's behavior throughout my childhood and early adulthood consisted of teasing and making fun of me, leaving me with the impression that he didn't truly see me for who I was. However, about six months ago, he unexpectedly opened up to me. He poured out his heart, acknowledging qualities in me that he had failed to recognize before. He admiringly said, "Candace, you are selfless and always ready to help others. You're a giver, seeking to bless everyone around you. You ask God for more so that you can continue to give." His heartfelt revelation concluded with, "It's very inspiring. I now understand why you are so blessed. You live to give, and that's truly remarkable." Moreover, he shared that God had been impressing upon him the importance of giving, helping others, and becoming a genuine example.

These moments with both my sister and brother solidified my belief that nothing I do is in vain. It's humbling to know that my actions and values have a positive impact on those around me, motivating them to embrace altruism and find their purpose. I'm grateful for the recognition and support, which further encourages me to stay true to my path of giving and making a difference in the lives of others.

Growing up, I admit I wasn't the best sister. Recognizing this, I made a conscious effort to improve my relationship with my siblings, and that required considerable work and dedication. My goal was to be effective not only in my professional life but also in my personal life, especially as a sister. As I underwent a transformation, I identified the areas I needed to work on and took deliberate steps to become a better sibling. I understand that many of us face challenges in getting along with our siblings, but I firmly believe that closeness can be achieved if we are willing to take the initiative. True effectiveness in building stronger sibling bonds begins with us, and I can attest to the positive impact it can have on our lives.

Consistency is key. You have to fight for the things you want and push until you get there. When you are tired, push; when you hurt, push; when you want to give up, push. Consistency is key!

God, when I struggle with being consistent, give me the strength I need to stay encouraged to push through. I pray that through all the distractions, I stay focused on the things you want me to accomplish. I pray I get to my destiny, and the empire I am building will be exactly what you want me to have because I trusted you, and I leaned on you by staying focused. God, I do not want to miss out on my blessings because I am distracted by temporary pleasures. Keep me focused, God.

Amen.

IMPROVE RELATIONSHIPS ON ALL ASPECTS OF THE SPECTRUM

Healthy relationships bring out the best in you.

Above all, love each other deeply, because love covers over a multitude of sins. Offer hospitality to one another without grumbling. Each of you should use whatever gift you have received to serve others, as faithful stewards of God's grace in its various forms.

—1 Peter 4:8–10 NIV

Relationships: A relationship is a dynamic connection between two individuals or groups, characterized by their emotions and behaviors towards each other. It extends beyond romantic entanglements and encompasses various aspects of life, such as bonds with parents, family, friends, colleagues, and significant others. Notably, relationships are not one-sided; they involve mutual efforts and understanding from both parties.

Personally, I faced challenges in this area due to some childhood barriers that affected my ability to form meaningful connections. I struggled to comprehend the essence of a relationship in any context. Looking back on my experiences, I believe that parents play a crucial role in shaping their children's understanding of relationships. They lay the foundation and serve as a blueprint for what healthy relationships should look like at home. However, if parents fail to provide this guidance, it becomes the individual's responsibility to recognize the significance of relationships and to define their own ideals for healthy connections.

Relationships are an essential aspect of life, influencing our emotional well-being and personal growth. Regardless of past difficulties, acknowledging their importance empowers us to actively cultivate and nurture these connections, fostering healthier and more fulfilling relationships with others.

With my mom being ill, my dad juggled work and tried his best to make life as normal as possible for us. Relationships were placed on the back burner, and we all entered survival mode, what I would call "autopilot." My siblings and I were left to learn how to love and keep others close on our own, as we were neither taught nor shown the importance of strong family bonds.

During the first seven years of my life, it was just my brother and me; we are two years apart in age. Observing my niece and nephew now, who are inseparable, I realize that my brother and I weren't as close when we were younger. In fact, we had our fair share of fistfights and wrestling matches. Throughout our adolescence, we didn't fully grasp the significance of having strong family ties or what that should look like for us. Arguments were a common occurrence when we spent time together, and we rarely stood up for each other.

In contrast, I had cousins with siblings who always had each other's backs. If one got into trouble, the others would step in to share the blame or prevent any from being placed solely on their sibling. However, my brother and I didn't have that kind of bond. If one of us got caught in a difficult situation, the other would often just laugh or walk away.

It wasn't until we both grew older and faced life's challenges that we started to develop a deeper connection. Now, I can proudly say that my brother is not only my sibling but also my friend. He has proven his unwavering support countless times, even offering me his last dollar when I was struggling financially. I remember times when I couldn't afford gas to get to work, and my little brother would come to my rescue, providing me with twenty or forty dollars to make sure I didn't go without.

Life's difficulties brought us together, and I cherish the strong bond we have now. My brother's willingness to be there for me has shown me the true meaning of family, and I am grateful for his presence in my life.

During a specific period in my early twenties, there was a routine where every Monday, I would call him to borrow forty dollars, promising to pay him back by Friday. Unfortunately, the cycle continued, and by the tenth time, he sat me down for a heart-to-heart conversation. "Candace," he said gently, "I'll always be here for you, but you need to improve your financial situation. Borrowing money every week isn't sustainable." His words resonated with me, and I knew he was right. That conversation marked the end of my constant requests for money.

At least, I believed it would be the last time I asked him for a financial favor. Regrettably, an entire year passed without us speaking,

despite living only thirty minutes apart in the same city. It was during this time that an incident occurred; I got pulled over by the police, and to my shock, I found out I had a warrant due to missed court dates for a speeding ticket. I was arrested, and my car was towed. Feeling desperate, the first person I called was my brother. Disappointment was evident in his eyes, but he came through with bail money. It pained me to realize that the only reason we reconnected was due to the traumas life had thrown my way after nearly a year of silence between us.

As adults, we make a conscious effort to maintain our connection, going above and beyond by driving or flying to visit each other, be it for special occasions or just to spend time together. My brother takes it upon himself to ensure his children recognize their aunty and build a bond with me. The relationship I share with him is truly beautiful, and I wouldn't trade him for anyone else, not in this lifetime or any other.

Sibling relationships are founded on being there for one another when it matters most. There was a time when he needed my support, and without divulging the details, let's just say I didn't hesitate to empty my bank account to ensure he was alright and could meet his needs. That's the essence of family – being there for each other through the best and the worst times, united through thick and thin.

It wasn't an easy journey; it took work, and it still does. Even after he bailed me out of jail, our bond didn't magically strengthen. My brother was deeply upset and disappointed, leading to a period of silence between us. In the end, I realized I had to be the bigger person and take the initiative. I picked up the phone and said, "Hey, how are you?" or asked if I could join him for lunch. I didn't want to be closer to friends than to my own blood. Not that there's anything wrong with that, but it wasn't the path I wanted to take. Family plays a crucial role in self-discovery. They can help you understand the reasons behind your actions and thoughts. Have you ever pondered why you are the way you are or why certain behaviors define you? Being around family can reveal the answers. My brother and I share many traits - hardworking, can-do attitude, resourceful, determined, loving, giving, and we achieve results. Spending just a short time with our extended family, one can easily connect the dots and see that we are all go-getters. As I grew older, I realized the significance of maintaining healthy relationships not only with my brother but also with my sister.

Regarding the relationship I had with my sister, I no longer regret not being a better sister because I have worked hard to establish a stronger bond with her. During our childhood, we became disconnected after starting off on a strong note. I treated her like my very own baby doll, always doing her hair and dressing her up – she was practically an extension of me. Wherever I went, my sister was right by my side, and my friends loved her just as much as I did.

There were many instances when I went above and beyond to ensure she had everything she needed. I vividly remember a particular prom night when she wanted a dress that cost $700, which felt like a fortune back then. Determined to help her, I approached my dad and proposed splitting the bill with him. Not only did I do that, but I also made sure her hair, lashes, and nails were taken care of – she meant the world to me.

Now, I am no longer burdened by regrets about the past, as I've put in the effort to strengthen our bond. We have overcome the disconnection, and our relationship has grown into something beautiful. It's heartwarming to see how much we've evolved and how much we mean to each other.

A year after prom, while I was away at college, my sister called me for help with buying clothes for her summer camp. Recognizing the importance of this for her, I wasted no time and secured a part-time job on campus to earn some money. Once back home, I joyfully took my baby girl along for the shopping spree, making it a memorable bonding experience for both of us.

I don't know when the disconnect happened, but as my sister got older and the years went by, she attended a university in Chicago. Despite living fewer than fifteen minutes from her apartment complex, we rarely spent time together. I can't help but feel I could have been an awesome big sister. Chicago is a beautiful city with so much to offer, and I missed countless opportunities for bonding. We could have explored the lakefront, rented a yacht for a day of fun, or simply had regular sleepovers to strengthen our bond. Looking back, I wish I had made more of an effort to connect with her during those years.

I could have been a better big sister. There's a seven-year age gap between us, and I realize now that she needed me more than I knew. But, truth be told, I needed her just as much. Unfortunately, I was too wrapped up in my own world, letting drama and selfishness consume me, leaving little room for anything or anyone else. It took time and maturity for me to step up and become the sister she deserved.

Now, I make a conscious effort to show her that I'm there for her, no matter what's going on in my life. We make sure to spend quality time together, going on trips, shopping, and simply hanging out and bonding whenever possible. It's heartwarming to see how much her children love me, and I've worked hard to build strong relationships with them. I want to be more than just an occasional aunt they see on holidays. In fact, they've even stayed with me for weeks during the summer, and we regularly connect through FaceTime, making our bond even stronger.

My sister and I are truly there for each other. We support, encourage, and pray for one another, which means a lot to both of us. It was an incredible moment when we talked about our sources of inspiration, and she confided in me that she looks up to me as a role model. She appreciates the woman I've become, someone who is loving, caring, and giving. I've experienced significant personal growth over the past years, and it's heartening to see that my sister has developed positive attributes too.

The connection we share is truly special, and I cherish every moment we spend together. It's so fulfilling to know that I can be an inspiration to my sister and play a meaningful role in her life.

Maintaining healthy relationships with my immediate family is of utmost importance to me. The family is a place where we are meant to experience love and learn how to extend that love to others. Therefore, I was determined not to let my adult years pass without having meaningful connections with my siblings. I made a conscious effort to be intentional about the relationships I cultivated within my family, and this positive approach also began to manifest in my relationships outside the family circle.

In my young-adult years, I struggled to maintain long-lasting relationships. Although I had friends in junior high with whom I initially connected well, our bond couldn't withstand the changes that came after high school graduation, and we all went our separate ways. Unlike some women who boasted about their enduring friendships, I found it challenging to keep a friend for more than a year.

I never lacked loyalty, love, generosity, or kindness in my friendships. The real struggle for me was staying connected with those who truly appreciated and accepted me for who I was, and having someone who could hold me accountable. After high school, I gained confidence in being true to myself and not allowing others to dictate my choices. This newfound independence caused me to drift apart from some friends who wanted to influence me differently.

My journey to building lasting relationships has been a mix of challenges and growth. I now understand the importance of staying true to myself while being open to forming connections with others who share similar values and goals. It's a continuous learning process, and I'm eager to embrace whatever comes my way in the future.

One of the main reasons my friendships haven't lasted long is my tendency to avoid confrontation. While I do stand up for myself and won't tolerate bullying, I struggle with addressing conflicts, especially when it involves being honest and speaking my mind. Confrontation feels uncomfortable, especially with those I genuinely love and care about.

Reflecting on a specific incident, a friend visited me in Chicago and stayed for a while. Since I wasn't working, she asked me to take her to work every day to avoid parking fees. Although we used her car, I didn't want to spend my summer solely on drop-offs and pickups, as I was still processing the fact that I had been terminated from a company I had worked at for years. Uncertain about my work situation, I decided to talk to her after a few drop-offs and expressed that I couldn't continue with the daily rides.

However, instead of being upfront and expressing my feelings and reasons, I avoided vulnerability and shut down communication. I realized that avoiding open communication was hindering my friendships. I couldn't continue living with the mindset that I'm always right, and when others are wrong, I simply walk away.

Moving forward, I understand the importance of open communication and honesty with my friends. I now recognize that disagreements are a natural part of any relationship, and addressing them constructively is crucial for fostering lasting and meaningful connections. It's a personal growth journey, and I'm committed to learning how to navigate conflicts and strengthen my friendships through understanding and empathy.

In my later adult years, I had a heartwarming reunion with a childhood friend whom I first met in kindergarten. This reconnection occurred in our thirties, and surprisingly, we became the best of friends. It's as if God wanted me to understand that life is better lived together, not alone. Undeniably, friendship is among life's most precious gifts, marked by unconditional love and mutual support.

Yet, I came to realize that genuine friendships don't come effortlessly; they require dedication and effort. I had experienced the tumultuous side of relationships throughout my teenage years, twenties, and even my early thirties, engaging in unhealthy dynamics where friends betrayed my trust, belittled me, and showed utter disrespect. I fought fervently for these toxic relationships, blinded by misguided determination.

However, as I entered this rekindled friendship, I learned an invaluable lesson. I had to make a conscious choice to invest in this bond, just as I had done in those harmful relationships. In this friendship, I've embraced vulnerability, honesty, and the willingness to accept feedback, even when it stings. The beauty of this connection lies in having someone to share life's journey with. Remarkably, my friend and I often find ourselves navigating through similar life experiences, allowing us to lend each other genuine understanding and support.

The path to a cherished friendship demands effort and growth, yet the rewards are immeasurable—having a companion to tackle life's highs and lows makes the journey all the more meaningful.

When I lived in Texas, I often found myself experiencing emotional struggles because I was single and still discovering the woman God intended me to be. Despite my friend not being in the same city, she was just a phone call away and provided much-needed affirmation that I was on the right path. Not only did she support me, but she also prayed for me during those challenging times.

True friendships are meant to uplift and hold us accountable. It's essential to have friends whom you can admire and learn from. A meaningful friendship should nourish your growth. If a friendship fails to contribute positively to your life and personal development, it may be worth reconsidering its significance. Honest communication and accountability are crucial in any friendship. If a friend is unable to be truthful with you or hold you accountable, it raises the question of whether that friendship truly adds value to your life.

Not everyone is meant to journey through life alongside you. It's easy to get caught up in the desire for friendships and connections, but it's essential to remember that these relationships should add value to your life on multiple levels.

We need healthy relationships. God did not intend for us to do life alone. Surround yourself not only with like-minded people but also with those who are wiser than you, those you can learn from, and those who will challenge and push you to become a better you!

God, send me my kind; send me my team. I want to grow and learn, so I can become better. That's one of the purposes of a healthy relationship. I know you want that for me; you want the best for me. Help me to forgive fast and be slow to become angry with my friends and family members. Help me to maintain healthy connections. You did not call us to do life alone. You want us to love others and do to others as you would have them do unto you.

Amen.

12

CHOOSING NOT TO TURN BACK: STAYING CONNECTED WITH WHO GOD CALLED YOU TO BE

*The road to destiny is not easy. In the
end, God will reward every tear.*

All of us, then, who are mature should take such
a view of things. And if on some point you think
differently, that too God will make clear to you. 16
Only let us live up to what we have already attained.
—Philippians 3:15–16 NIV

"Run, sis, run!" I sprinted, keeping the pace, and refusing to look back. Why? Because my deepest desire was to remain connected and aligned with the will of God. I had spent my entire life doing things my way, which only led me to a life of destruction, failure, and constant struggle. Living in a world of chaos, I found myself on the altar every Sunday, asking God for forgiveness for the same mistakes, week after week after week. I share this not to judge anyone else, for I was once that girl.

I was the girl who found herself in a guy's bedroom one moment and back on the altar the next Sunday. I had a foul mouth and a limited vocabulary, yet there I was, back on the altar, asking for redemption. Lies, manipulation, and disloyalty were traits that characterized me. But now, I stand here, having finally reached a place where I wholeheartedly crave God's presence in my life, desiring His guidance at every step of the way.

After praying that short yet simple prayer, there was no turning back for me. Leaving Chicago became the reset I desperately needed. I relocated to Louisiana, determined to face the challenges with courage, shedding tears and fighting my way to align with God's plan for me. I understood that anything worth fighting for wouldn't come easily, but I trusted that God would support me every step of the way. I made a conscious decision to fight for my faith in God.

Louisiana holds a special place in my heart, as it is where I discovered God and established a connection with Him. I built a spiritual altar as a gesture of surrendering myself entirely to God, symbolizing a fresh start. "Hello, God, it's Candace. I acknowledge that in the past, I regretfully did not choose you, but now, I wholeheartedly commit to following your path. I deeply apologize for relying on my own ways, and I earnestly desire to embrace you as the guiding force in my life."Choosing not to look back and revert to old ways is an incredibly challenging journey. However, it is on this path that one discovers the true abundance of blessings waiting on the other side. I wholeheartedly sought forgiveness with a pure heart, and remarkably, within thirty days, a promotion awaited me. Embracing God's guidance didn't make my life exempt from grief and heartache, but it did fill it with wins and good days. On the tough days, I found solace in leaning on God's unwavering support and finding comfort in His embrace while navigating the growing pains.

Since I committed myself to walk this path with God, my life has undergone a profound transformation. My thoughts, speech, and sensitivity towards others have evolved, shedding the shackles of pride, greed, and lust that once bound me. My perspective on everything has shifted, and my mind is now clear and focused.

As I previously mentioned, surrendering to God doesn't mean life becomes devoid of challenges. Instead, it means having God as your steadfast companion, walking beside you through every difficulty. Just six months after my promotion, while in Baton Rouge, I faced death threats fueled by resentment from long-time employees who had never been held accountable or had someone to lead and guide them effectively.

Despite the hardships, my faith in God helped me endure these trials. I held onto the belief that with God's support, I could weather any storm. And so can you, dear reader, for embracing God's presence and guidance transforms lives and gives the strength to triumph over adversity.

After working at the store in Louisiana, for six months, I received shocking news that it was closing down, leaving all employees, including leaders, displaced and in need of interviewing for positions elsewhere. The countless hours of hard work I invested to transform the store from a "red store" to a "green store" suddenly seemed uncertain. Initially, I spiraled into negative thoughts, fearing unemployment and uncertainty looming over me. However, in that moment, I reminded myself of the God I served— a protector and provider who desires happiness and showers blessings upon us.

With this realization, my perspective on the situation shifted. Though the employment outlook seemed uncertain, I found comfort in knowing I was protected and free from worry or fear with God by my side. Supportive family members, including aunts and uncles, reached out to my dad to inquire about my well-being and career status. While I was indeed affected, my faith as a woman of God kept me grounded and reassured that I would be taken care of. I entrusted all my worries and anxiety to God, allowing faith to guide me through this challenging time.

This experience serves as a powerful example that being a Christian and doing the right things doesn't guarantee immunity from difficulties. Life's challenges will inevitably arise, but the beauty of choosing God is that He stands by our side, carrying us through tough times. His grace and favor granted me strength and resilience.

Unbeknown to me, the company had already set a position aside for me in Texas - one of their busiest stores. Not only was the salary more substantial, but there was also a tempting signing bonus awaiting me. It was an opportunity that seemed heaven-sent, and I chose to put my trust in God for it to work out. I entrusted Him to take care of my employment and financial worries, and I decided not to be deterred by any controversy or conflict that came my way. By doing so, God pulled me through and handled everything with perfect control. In hindsight, it appears that I ran towards a better future by wholeheartedly choosing God's path. My journey took me from Chicago to Baton Rouge and then to Texas, each move driven by the desire for God's best in my life.

Over the last decade and more, I've witnessed God elevate me through various promotions. It's a rewarding experience that comes from choosing to follow Him. Throughout the ups and downs, God has always provided for me, ensuring that all my needs are met. So, I encourage you to place your trust in God - you won't be left wanting. Trust in Him, and you won't have to endure any lack.

I embraced Texas with a resounding "yes." It became a sacred space where I delved into my spiritual journey, forging a connection with God and honing my ability to discern His voice. Clarity washed over me, revealing my purpose and its unique manifestation in my life. Simultaneously, I was employed at one of the company's most bustling stores, and I took on the challenge with unyielding determination.

The echoes of "run, sis, run" reverberated in my mind. From that moment, I never looked back. Peace enveloped me, and as I reminisce, I label that period as my "grinding season." Not only did I discover my purpose in Texas, but I also managed to fortify my financial standing significantly, laying a stable foundation for the journey ahead. Such preparation would prove vital for the endeavors awaiting me in the near future.

When you are in alignment with God, a transformation occurs within you. Your taste buds undergo a shift, and your wants and desires undergo a profound change because you become attuned to seeking what God has destined for you. Essentially, living life according to God's will leads to a harmonization of desires, where your aspirations align with His divine purpose, and His wishes become your own. I had been diligently saving and paying down my debt in an effort to boost my credit score. Little did I know that in just a matter of months, I would find myself in a situation where I needed both a considerable amount of money and an exceptional credit score to achieve my next.

"Run, sis, run, and don't look back. By continuously moving forward without glancing behind, you remain aligned with the will of God. While God can guide you back on track if you deviate from the plan, staying prepared means you never have to worry about getting ready. Your life is now flowing in harmony with God's desires, eliminating the need for starting over. Keep following this path, and you'll continue to live your life in the way God intends."

As I embraced a life aligned with God's will, I noticed a profound shift in my taste buds. It stirred a deep sense that transformation was on the horizon. Although unsure of the exact path that lay ahead, I sensed the need for something new in my life. During my stay in Texas, I dedicated my days to forging a closer connection with God and earnestly sought His guidance for my role in His kingdom. Through this journey, God revealed a purpose for me, and I realized it was now my responsibility to pursue it with unwavering determination.

Since a stirring in my spirit signaled the need for change, I decided to explore the idea of pursuing a career that aligned with my true purpose. I took the initiative to update my résumé and actively seek new opportunities. Although I received several job offers, I turned them down because they didn't offer the salary I desired. While it's true that sometimes taking a step back can lead to a major comeback, that approach didn't resonate with where I currently stood in life. I believed that God had called me to elevate, and it was my responsibility to remain steadfast in that direction. In the past, I had taken steps back and eventually found my way forward, but this time, I knew I needed to listen to God's guidance above all else.

Time passed, and in my heart, I became certain that I had heard God's calling regarding my purpose and what He wanted me to pursue. Strikingly, it had little connection to my current profession. I strongly sensed that I was destined to lead, to be an exemplar, and to empower women. My mission was to show them their true potential, guiding them towards a profound relationship with God, and incorporating Him into every facet of their lives.

I opened my mind and started to think differently. After nearly nineteen years of working for the same company, I realized it was time for a career change that would better align with the woman I had become. Although the idea excited me, I couldn't deny feeling a bit anxious, as my current role and company had been my comfort zone for so long. However, I was determined to trust in the path that God had in store for me and move forward with confidence.

The timing of events was truly remarkable, that's how God works. Just days after reaching this mental readiness for change, I received an unexpected call at 6 a.m. from a good friend. He informed me that there were available positions in the company he currently worked for. It seemed like divine intervention, a clear sign that I should explore this opportunity and consider it as part of God's plan for my career transition.

Run, Candace, run, and don't look back. I interviewed, received an offer, and gladly accepted it, prompting my move to Atlanta. Upon arrival, I already knew in my heart who God had called me to be. This clear sense of purpose empowered me to start living intentionally, positioning myself to hear and discern God's plan for the purpose He bestowed upon me. I diligently avoided becoming complacent or overly comfortable, recognizing that, despite the great things happening, God always has more in store for us.

Truly blessed, I am often left in awe and amazement by the wonders God has bestowed upon me. I have been fortunate enough to rent a beautiful home conveniently close to my job. Each day, I remind myself to stay focused, urging myself on with the words, "Stay determined, Candace, and embrace the path God has set for you. Only then can you become the person He intended you to be, and there are countless bigger and greater days awaiting you.

In Atlanta, I received a divine strategy that revealed the beginning of my true purpose. Amidst this newfound clarity, God presented me with choices: to either embrace the familiar persona of my past self, the Candace I was during my young-adult years in Chicago, or to heed His call and become the person He intended me to be. While it's easier to stay focused when surrounded by limited distractions, Atlanta offered a multitude of temptations—from lavish indulgences like shopping, dining, and entertainment to more enticing vices like strip clubs and lounges. Having spent almost seven years in places with fewer distractions, like Baton Rouge and Texas, I found myself captivated by Georgia's abundance.

However, I made a conscious decision to remain faithful and keep my eyes fixed on God's promise. I was determined not to be blindsided by the allure of this new city, state, and lifestyle. Instead, I took on the challenge with unwavering resolve. Reflecting on my past, I realized that living in sin and following my own desires had only led to disappointment and frustration. But since I started living in accordance with God's will, I've witnessed incredible growth and progress in my life, making it clear that I can't afford to regress.

So, I ran with determination, refusing to look back. Georgia became both a gift and a test from God, a sign that I was ready to embrace true freedom. It was His way of saying, "Candace, the time has come for you to be truly free. Now, let's see what you'll do with this freedom." Admittedly, the journey wasn't effortless, but in the end, I chose to walk with God wholeheartedly.

Leaving Chicago to pursue personal growth may not have seemed like the best decision initially, but looking back, it turned out to be the most significant choice I've ever made. I often wonder how different my life would have been if I hadn't taken that leap of faith and left. In Louisiana, I found a deep connection with God, investing genuine and wholehearted effort to get to know Him better. Texas became the place where I sought God's voice, seeking purpose and quieting my heart to discern His plan for me. The time spent there enabled me to lead a life that pleases God. In Georgia, I received invaluable strategy and knowledge on how to fulfill my purpose. Despite having the means and opportunities to be whoever I wanted, I consciously chose to embrace God's calling and dedicated myself to developing my purpose. My intention was to be a blessing to others and become a vessel through which God could work on Earth.

Choosing not to turn back and to stay connected with who God has called you to be isn't a simple decision. We all have questions for which answers may elude us. How do you maintain your focus and resist the temptation to regress? What if I make mistakes? What happens when I stumble? Remember, if you do falter, have faith in God's love and forgiveness. When you err, acknowledge it, and then pick up where you left off, continuing to move forward. Sincerity and proactive change form the foundation of staying connected to the path God has chosen for you.

Would I have to start over? No, you don't have to start over from scratch. Walking with God is not like an exam. When you fail, you have to start over. You get up and keep going. The beauty of walking with God is that he forgives and wants us to have the desires of our hearts. It's totally up to you to get there. If you want what God has for you, do your best every day. Don't give up. Don't go back to old habits.

As I mentioned earlier, I had to go cold turkey, and the hardest thing to do was to change my circle. I couldn't hang out with the same group of friends. They didn't change, so I had to make a change. Every question drove anxiety and caused me to put unnecessary pressure on myself.

Staying where you are and not regressing requires effort. It all starts with keeping your focus on the promise. I firmly believe that God has a purpose for me and has shown me what my future holds. Taking delight in the Lord and staying aligned with His will became my guiding principle. Identifying our weaknesses and recognizing what tempts us to take a step back is crucial. Whatever triggers you might have, self-awareness is key, and it's essential to avoid those triggers. For me, it meant completely cutting out alcohol from my lifestyle. I was well aware of its negative effects on me – making me reckless, unaware, and vulnerable. This vulnerability led me to engage in behavior I later regretted. Moreover, alcohol would drag me into depression. Knowing it was a trigger, I made a conscious effort to stay away from it and remained focused on my goals.

What keeps me focused is holding onto the promise that God has for me. Through divine guidance, I have gained a profound understanding of my true identity and the boundless potential within me. My unwavering determination is directed towards reaching my full potential, knowing that my current state is not where God intends for me to remain indefinitely. Throughout this journey with God, I can proudly acknowledge the tremendous progress I have made. The path to this point demanded significant effort and a complete transformation of my life. By embracing consistency, I continue to stay aligned with God's will and fulfill the purpose to which He has called me.

Allow God to mold you, bend you, and allow pain and hurt to create the woman he is forming you to be. I know it doesn't feel good, but to get to your destiny, the pain must flow; you have to go through it. Allow God to use you. Stop running. Embrace it, and watch what God has for you in the end!

God, keep my mind and my thoughts pure. Keep me focused. When I am tempted to revert to old ways and old habits, keep my mind focused on you. As I create the space and time to bond with you, give me the strength I need to face the world and reality. Help others to see Christ when they see me, and because of how I am living, God, I pray they want to get to know you on an intimate level. God, I want you to get the glory. I desire you and everything you have for me and my life.

Amen.

13

FINANCIAL STEWARDSHIP AND GIVING

You have to shift your mindset to maintain wealth.

———————————

The wise store up choice food and olive oil, but fools gulp theirs down.

—Proverbs 21:20 NIV

There is an old saying: "If you stay prepared, you won't need to prepare." This principle extends to your finances too. The truly prudent manage to acquire both prosperity and luxury. Have you considered what steps you're taking to not just amass wealth for yourself, but to secure generational wealth? If this question makes you uncomfortable, it could indicate that you haven't yet established a solid financial foundation. Don't fret or feel guilty if you find yourself lagging behind; everyone's journey is different. Perhaps this hasn't been your narrative, but there might be someone you know who could benefit from some encouragement and guidance. I, too, once found myself in that position, but with determination and effort, I managed to turn things around.

Yes, that was indeed me. I was the girl who didn't put herself in a good financial position. My financial irresponsibility and procrastination were evident, and I'm owning up to it. Recently, my cousin and I had a good laugh as we reminisced about the past. Here we are now, both in our thirties, and things have changed for the better. We always knew that financial literacy was important, but we didn't fully grasp the significance of budgeting and saving until later on. While we understood the importance of paying bills on time and maintaining good credit, we struggled to put that knowledge into practice.

Now, however, we have both come a long way and are doing quite well. We've learned from our mistakes, and our credit scores have improved significantly. My cousin recently said to me, "Candace, what were we thinking back then? Why were we so irresponsible with our finances? We didn't realize how much we were setting ourselves back." Hearing her words, I couldn't help but laugh because she was absolutely right.

The journey to financial responsibility has been a learning experience, but I'm glad we finally got on the right track. We now understand that knowing better doesn't always lead to doing better. However, our past mistakes have taught us valuable lessons, and we are committed to making smarter financial decisions moving forward.

After graduating from high school, I promptly obtained my first credit card with a $500 credit limit. However, my initial financial decision-making left much to be desired. I impulsively maxed out the card in no time. Although I managed to make the first two payments on schedule, my lack of discipline soon caught up with me as I became too negligent to mail in the monthly checks. I acknowledge that the responsibility falls solely on my shoulders, as I had no one to guide me on proper financial stewardship and stress its significance. In all honesty, I was aware of the fundamentals; it's essentially Economics 101. Borrowing money comes with the obligation to repay it in a timely manner, and even if you cannot settle the full amount, making the minimum payment is essential. It's a straightforward concept that I should have practiced more diligently.

Life has a way of becoming complicated, and often, we find ourselves in situations that set us back. However, it doesn't always have to be this way. Looking back, I realize there were numerous instances where I could have prevented such setbacks. Despite having common sense when it came to managing my finances, I sometimes overlooked simple calculations. For instance, when earning $4,000 per month and paying $1,200 in rent, I had $2,800 left to cover utility bills, gas, and food expenses. Being more mindful of these basic calculations could have helped me avoid unnecessary financial difficulties. If I had made the effort to create a budget, I could have avoided the issues I encountered. I understand that not everyone is guilty of neglecting a budget, but I certainly was. Budgeting doesn't require a complex scientific approach. It's as simple as jotting down your monthly income, listing all your expenses, and then subtracting the expenses from your income. The remaining amount can be either saved or spent. The responsible choice would be to save the surplus. It's genuinely that straightforward.

During a certain phase in my life, I found myself constantly borrowing gas money from my brother every two weeks. Eventually, he confronted me about my situation, urging me to pull myself together. Another incident that stands out is the night I spent with my boyfriend, only to run out of gas the next morning while he headed to work. I was deeply embarrassed by the predicament and felt too ashamed to call him for help, not just because of running out of gas, but because I had no money to refuel my Cadillac. With a heavy heart, I decided to leave my car on the side of the road and walk to the nearest gas station, which was a humbling experience in the early hours of the morning.

As I reached the gas station, I had to gather my courage to approach a stranger and ask for money to buy gas. The way he looked at me made me feel incredibly small, not with disgust, but with disappointment. Despite living a life that wasn't necessarily aligned with my values, he saw something in me that exuded greatness. There I was, standing tall, confident, and well-presented with a designer handbag, yet humbly requesting money from a stranger to fill my tank.

To my surprise, the kind-hearted stranger agreed to help and gave me the money I needed. He even went the extra mile by driving me back to my car and assisting me in filling up the tank. This encounter left a profound impact on me, making me reflect on the choices I was making in life and the importance of humility and gratitude.

It was my fault. All I had to do was budget. I was careless. Every time I got paid, I thought I had money to spare, and I just spent it without considering the consequences. I should have been more responsible and created a budget. Like everyone else, I've made careless and irresponsible decisions that negatively impacted my finances and credit. In my early twenties, I used to spend every night at my aunt and uncle's house. The only issue was that their suburb had strict parking regulations, and cars were not allowed to park on the street overnight. If you wanted to park on the street, you had to inform the authorities by making a quick phone call. It sounds simple, but somehow, I couldn't find those couple of minutes to make the call. As a result, I ended up getting a ticket every single night I stayed over. Before I knew it, I had accumulated $5,000 in fines. I must admit, calling myself careless and irresponsible might be an understatement in this situation.

It is within our power to make responsible financial choices. By doing so, we ensure preparedness for the future and seize opportunities when they arise. Maintaining a healthy credit line and sound finances ensures that we have resources readily available. The best part is that even if your credit is currently unfavorable, it is possible to repair it. Contrary to what many believe, improving your credit score is achievable with the right steps and dedication.

As I matured and climbed the corporate ladder, I began to challenge myself with a realization: "Candace, you can't be making a six-figure salary and have bad credit." Despite holding a great job with an impressive income for my age, I was unable to utilize it fully due to my credit situation. As an adult, I even had to rely on my dad to cosign for an apartment, which was disheartening. If only I had been more responsible with my credit and paid my bills on time, I could have easily secured my own place.

Establishing and maintaining good credit shouldn't be complicated; it's not rocket science. I vividly recall the stress of maxing out my credit cards and feeling overwhelmed by the debts I had accumulated on each one. In truth, all I needed to do was pay the minimum balance on time. Although maxing out the cards did negatively impact my credit score, consistently paying bills on time would have led to a quick recovery once the debts were settled.

Finally, I reached a point of accountability and decided to be intentional about getting out of debt and repairing my credit. Taking matters into my hands, I made calls to every debtor and started paying off each debt methodically, one at a time, until I was debt-free.

As Christians, it's crucial to recognize the interconnection of every aspect of our lives. It all begins with the decision to align our lives with God's will and surrender every part of ourselves, including our financial matters, to Him. Neglecting our financial responsibilities contradicts our commitment to being followers of God. Maintaining good financial stewardship is an essential part of living a consistent and faithful life.

When I surrendered my life to Christ, I experienced a profound sense of honesty and conviction in all areas, including my finances. It's my aspiration as a Christian to strive to become the best version of myself, wholly dedicated to God. This conviction becomes a guiding light, motivating us to excel on all levels and live in accordance with God's plan.

Let us remember that our actions, including how we manage our finances, reflect our commitment to God and His teachings. By being responsible and honoring our financial obligations, we demonstrate our faithfulness to God and His blessings in our lives.

Doing this for God also means I am doing it for others as well. By demonstrating what it means to have a solid financial standing with God, I create an opportunity for God's influence to manifest in the earthly realm through my actions. Romans 13:7 (NIV) emphasizes the importance of fulfilling our obligations, such as paying taxes, rendering revenue, and showing respect and honor to those who deserve it. Biblically, we are called to be responsible and accountable for our finances, including our credit.

Over the past several years, I have dedicated myself to cultivating a strong relationship with God. One of the significant changes I made was taking greater responsibility for my finances. This involved obtaining my credit report and diligently paying off each debt one by one, until I finally achieved the liberating state of being debt-free. I came to understand that credit plays an essential role in modern life, as it is tied to our financial reputation.

Coincidentally, as I started my journey to financial freedom, I had no idea that a relocation was on the horizon. As God would have it, I needed good credit to rent a home in Georgia. This realization only reaffirmed my belief that being connected with God aligned me with His will. It became clear to me that moving was part of God's plan for my life, and thus, my determination to pay off my debts took on even greater significance.

I witnessed the fruits of my efforts when my credit score significantly improved, crossing the 700 mark in just a matter of months. Embracing God's guidance, I also adopted a disciplined approach to saving money. Even when tempted by trips and shopping sprees, I resisted the urge and focused on my financial goals. This commitment allowed me to pay off my debts entirely and reach the highest credit score I had ever achieved. Moreover, I managed to amass substantial savings, totaling thousands of dollars.

My journey of faith and financial growth has been deeply rewarding. As I look back on my progress, I am filled with gratitude for the alignment of my actions with God's will, leading me to a place of financial security and peace.

One early morning, I woke up to a text inquiring whether I would be interested in relocating to another state. Without hesitation, I gladly accepted the offer, knowing that it presented an opportunity for a higher salary. To make this relocation possible, I had to rely on the money I had diligently saved and the efforts I put into repairing my credit. Had I not been proactive in improving my credit and saving up, I wouldn't have been prepared when the call came.

This is where my faith and relationship with God came full circle. By surrendering all aspects of my life to Him and living according to His will, I believe God guided me in the right direction. He revealed His plan for my life and prepared me for the promotion that awaited me. It was as if God knew the call was coming and instilled in me the motivation to work on my professional and financial growth. When you trust God with every area of your life, He will provide you with the guidance and wisdom to align yourself with His purpose for you.

The promotion I received was more than just a career advancement; it was a testament to the power of faith and the importance of aligning myself with God's plan. I am grateful for this journey and for the way God works in mysterious but incredible ways. Now, I look forward to this new chapter, knowing that God's hand is leading the way.

When I moved to Georgia, I knew I wouldn't buy a home right away. My plan was to familiarize myself with the state and its surrounding suburbs before making such a significant decision. Thus, I opted to rent a home near my workplace, and consequently, I completed a rental application. It was a comforting feeling to discover that my credit was in excellent condition and that I had more than enough funds to secure the rental through a deposit. I can't even begin to imagine the challenges I might have faced or the potential homes I might have missed out on if I hadn't been adequately prepared. Thankfully, I was ready for this step, and all I had to do was say "yes" to get there, knowing I had made the necessary preparations.

Financial stewardship encompasses the act of giving, which God encourages us to do willingly and joyfully. I've always had a natural inclination to give and share, but before surrendering my life to Christ, I must admit that I was somewhat self-absorbed, often neglecting the needs of others unintentionally. My focus was primarily on myself, and others ended up being last on my list of priorities.

However, when I surrendered my life to God, I experienced a profound transformation, including a conviction about my finances. I have numerous heartwarming stories related to the blessings of giving. Whether it was contributing to the spiritual ministry that nurtured me or following God's prompting to support others, I found immense joy in giving. The feeling of giving is genuinely gratifying, especially since I can discern God's voice as a believer.

One instance stands out vividly in my memory when I heard God telling me to give a friend $150. Although I hesitated initially, due to being influenced by my human desires rather than the Spirit, I eventually fulfilled His calling. Interestingly, the very next day, my friend unexpectedly reached out to borrow exactly $150. I was overjoyed to be able to help her without hesitation.

Through my journey of financial stewardship and giving, I've come to understand the significance of being a cheerful giver, as it brings both blessings to others and a sense of fulfillment within me.

In that moment of excitement, there was also a tinge of sadness, as I realized I hadn't heeded God's voice. Instead, I allowed my own thoughts to cloud my judgment, thinking, "Candace, don't offer people money. What if they question your intentions or perceive you as arrogant, acting like a Goody Two-shoes, just handing out money?" Regrettably, I ignored God's prompting to give and hesitated until she asked.

Although I felt joy in giving, my reluctance took away its beauty, and, more importantly, it disconnected me from God's purpose. That experience served as a profound lesson for me. I don't want to interfere with what God is doing on this earth; I desire to be a willing vessel for His blessings, sharing them with others selflessly. Giving comes naturally to me, and it brings me genuine joy. My intentions are pure; I never give with the expectation of receiving something in return. I give because I genuinely want to share and help others.

When I am out, I always seek opportunities to be a blessing to others. Whether I'm at a grocery store or among my loved ones, friends, or family, my heart is set on giving back.

Maintaining a relationship with Christ is far from a one-size-fits-all experience. Each person's walk with God is unique and personal. What God calls me to do may be entirely different from what He calls someone else to do. For instance, there have been instances when I felt led to spontaneously pay for the person in front of or behind me at the grocery store. Moreover, there were times when I joyfully donated $10,000 to a ministry that profoundly enriched me spiritually, or to someone whom God specifically directed me to support. In those moments, I never questioned God's guidance, but rather embraced the opportunity to give with a willing heart.

Giving back to Christ is the least we can do to show our gratitude. From an early age, I was taught to follow the 10 percent rule, which is rooted in the verse from Leviticus 27:30 NIV, stating that a tithe of everything from the land belongs to the Lord. This practice served as a constant reminder that all we have ultimately comes from God, and it is an act of appreciation to give a portion of it back to Him. Offering 10 percent is a way of expressing thanks for the blessings we've received and acknowledging His role in our lives. It's a modest gesture that symbolizes our recognition of His presence and generosity.

If it is placed on my heart to give more than 10 percent, I do not hesitate to give. I understand that giving generously does not mean going without, rather, it is an act of faith that ensures abundance will always flow. Allow me to share a remarkable example of this belief in action. Recently, the time came for me to purchase my home, despite being single and without children. My desire was to not only create a home for myself but also to set an example for my family – to demonstrate what wonders God can manifest when one aligns their life with His will and remains committed.

To ensure I was financially prepared for this significant step, I diligently paid off all my debts and worked on maintaining an excellent credit score. I was also mindful of saving money, knowing that a substantial deposit would be necessary. Thanks to thorough research and networking with people in the real estate industry, I had amassed more than enough funds and was confident that I was in the perfect position to buy my first home.

Upon returning to Georgia from visiting family out of town, I was ready to proceed with my plan. I intended to reach out to my real estate agent and ask her to connect me with her preferred lender. This would help me determine how much I could be approved for, and I would then base my house-hunting efforts around that figure.

I was immediately preapproved for the amount I would need. After reviewing my account, she gave me my budget and told me to start looking. My real estate agent sent me a list of homes, and one of them caught my eye. It had everything on my wish list—a beautiful kitchen, high ceilings, fireplaces, a sitting room, and another fireplace in the owners' suite. My real estate agent found my dream home, located in one of the most prestigious communities in southern Georgia. However, to my dismay, it was over my budget.

My real estate agent promptly contacted the seller's agent to inquire about the price. Surprisingly, we learned that the price of the home had gone down that very morning. It felt like divine intervention!

With this new development, the house became more affordable and within my reach. I truly believed that this home was meant to be mine; I could feel it in my spirit. God was making a way for me.

Filled with excitement, I decided to put in an offer for the home. However, during a discussion with the lender, she informed me that I needed to bring more money to the closing table. I couldn't help but wonder, "God, why do I need more money? I've diligently paid off my debts and ensured that I had more than enough for a down payment. Why are the stakes changing now?"

Despite the unexpected challenge, I remained hopeful and determined. I knew that if God had opened this door for me, He would provide a solution. I began exploring different options to secure the additional funds, all the while holding onto the belief that this home was indeed meant to be mine.

The lender's words echoed in my ears, "Candace, I can get you closed in fourteen days if you can get your hands on the additional capital by then." Without a moment's hesitation, I replied with a resolute "yes." My faith in God was unwavering; I firmly believed He would not forsake me. Giving and tithing had always been an integral part of my life, and I trusted that blessings would come my way.

As God would have it, my lease was expiring, and new tenants were already lined up by the owners. The timing seemed pressing, but deep within, I felt a calling to own a place of my own, and I was determined to stick to what I believed God had communicated to me. Soon, I discovered a home that resonated with my heart. Initially beyond my budget, it miraculously underwent a price reduction, bringing it within my financial reach. However, additional liquid cash was still required.

Throughout this process, one thing remained constant: my unwavering belief that God would intervene and work everything out for me.

I made another offer on the home. After ending the call, I found myself saying, "Okay, Candace, you have to find additional capital within two weeks. I really need some divine intervention here." I turned to prayer: "God, I don't know where this money is going to come from, but I truly need it within two weeks."

My cousin asked me, "Girl, what are you going to do? Are you going to try to save more money and try again next year?" I told her, "Absolutely not." I was determined to secure this home and close the deal within two weeks. I had faith that God would work everything out in my favor.

I would have normally kept my financial challenge close to the vest. But I have learned to listen to God's voice as it pertains to absolutely everything. For whatever reason, I felt it was OK to share. I honestly felt the need to be honest and vulnerable enough to share what I needed God to do for me. I needed a miracle! I was not sure how God was going to do it, but I believed he was going to make it happen for me. Every day I went to the mailbox in expectation. I expected that the additional money was going to be there.

One day, I was on the phone with my sister, and she asked about my progress and how things were going. I shared with her that I had found my dream home, but I needed additional funds for the down payment. Without hesitation, she offered her support, saying, "Girl, I'll help you out. Just let me know how you want me to send it. It might not cover the full amount, but I can definitely contribute."

Later on, my aunt called, inquiring about my house hunting journey, and I informed her that things were going well, except for a financial hurdle I had encountered. To my surprise, she said, "Candace, I can't help directly, but your cousin can." And indeed, my cousin stepped in to offer assistance.

During a conversation with my best friend, she expressed her heartfelt desire to help, but she wasn't able to provide financial support. However, she assured me that her boyfriend was more than willing to help without any prompting from her. It was in these moments of my loved ones willingly giving without me even asking that I realized the hand of God working through them.

The generosity and kindness shown by my sister, aunt, and best friend affirmed to me that divine intervention was at play, orchestrating these acts of generosity in my life.

When my real estate agent found out that I had managed to come up with the money, her immediate response was, "Candace, your family doesn't mess around when it comes to supporting you." Yet, in that moment, all I could think about was how God has been unwavering in His support for me. I have always been intentional about giving back to others, never doing so reluctantly. Tithing is a crucial aspect of my life, and when the time came for me to receive blessings in return, not only did I get back what I had given, but I also received even more.

That's the beauty of giving. Luke 6:38 (NIV) says, "Give, and it shall be given to you; good measure, pressed down, and shaken together, and running over, shall men give into your bosom." That is exactly what happened. People gave. People gave willingly to my bosom. I wonder what would happen if I didn't give, if I did not tithe. Yes, God is a God with both mercy and grace. He extends us favor, but it honestly would not have been that simple. I was able to breathe amid my financial turmoil. I was able to give my financial concern to God and walk away from it. God worked it out for me. When you sow, it's like you are investing in your future. You're storing up blessings for when you need them. When I was in need, I did not have to beg or ask. People gave.

I successfully closed on my new home just two weeks after making an offer. The power of generosity not only brought down the price of the house but also encouraged people to contribute willingly. Embrace the blessings that God has in store for you and never miss out on them. Giving can truly enrich your life and make a positive impact.

a better you
EXPERIENCE

Nothing about your
past defines your
future.

You define it.

Success is in
your hands.

Wealth is in your
hands.

God, I know you want each of us to be wealthy in every possible way—health, peace of mind, and material possessions. God, I know you want this for me, not just for my sake, but for the sake of all humankind. I know you want me to be blessed, God, and I also want to be a blessing to others. I want to be blessed so I can help others. God, please continue to instill in me the importance of financial stewardship and giving. As long as I give consistently, I will never go without.

Amen.

14

THE CONCLUSION

Fixing the broken in me, that's self-love.

Love is patient, love is kind. It does not envy, it does not boast, it is not proud. It does not dishonor others, it is not self-seeking, it is not easily angered, it keeps no record of wrongs.

—1 Corinthians 13:4–5 NIV

Self-love: Embracing every aspect of who I am, cherishing my well-being and happiness. It involves tending to my needs and priorities without compromising them to appease others. Self-love empowers me to resist settling for anything less than I truly deserve.

I embrace myself amidst the loneliness and through the tears. I've learned to love myself even during times of brokenness, as I tend to my wounds and find comfort within. Regardless of where life places me, I still love and cherish myself, just as Christ loves me. At times, God's plans may not seem clear or pleasant, but I have spent years evolving into the woman I am today. Embracing God's love has led me to love myself unconditionally, taking care of all aspects of my being. His love is eternal, unwavering, and faithful. When the world turns its back on us, God remains, embracing us with open arms. If God loves me without conditions, I should also love and respect myself in the same way, meeting God where He is. In the past, I may have lived recklessly, following my own desires rather than God's will. Recognizing my worth, I knew the aspects I needed to work on, fueled by my deep love for myself. This self-love guided me away from a destructive path, and I made the choice to live a life that aligns with my true self.

I embarked on a journey of immediate self-improvement and committed myself to consistency. Following God's guidance, I understood that abstinence was the first step to take. Engaging in casual relationships without preserving myself for marriage only led to unnecessary hardships. My heart was burdened with pain and brokenness, and I grew weary of living life on my terms. I made the mistake of giving myself to men who didn't see me as their life partner and lacked genuine intentions. Time after time, I surrendered my body and soul, but what remained after the fleeting pleasure was loneliness and singlehood. It became clear that I should reserve my body for my future husband, as an expression of self-love and respect. I have now taken charge of my life, refusing to be deceived or manipulated by men. Instead, I have entrusted my heart to God, finding safety and security in His care.

Whenever I find myself on the brink of giving up, I draw strength from the boundless love that God has for me. His love knows no bounds, and He patiently waits for me to approach Him, no matter how broken or imperfect I feel. God's acceptance of me as I am gives me hope, and His grace grants me another chance to grow and improve. It's a reminder that I should love myself just as Christ loves me, unconditionally and without judgment.

Embracing this love empowers me to strive for a better future. I am determined to invest effort in my personal growth and well-being. As I do so, a sense of liberation envelops me. My mind becomes clearer, unburdened by doubts and fears, allowing me to tackle the challenges that lie ahead with renewed vigor.

In this journey of self-improvement, I am not alone. God's love supports me, and I find comfort in knowing that I am never abandoned. With His guidance, I can confront all that concerns me and continue to progress in life.

Loving yourself also requires facing the challenges that hold you back from achieving greatness. For generations, my family has been bound by generational curses that hindered us from fulfilling our true potential, blocking us from the path God intended. Depression became a severe struggle for me, leading me to seek solace in alcohol to numb the pain. I understood that to attain mental clarity, I had to achieve physical sobriety first. Recognizing that depression was slowly consuming me, I made the decision to seek God's guidance to overcome it. At times, I felt overwhelmed, and I found myself self-pitying and isolating as an introvert. During moments of turmoil, I felt like my world was collapsing around me.

When I made the decision to align my life and lifestyle with God's will, I experienced a profound sense of lightness. I've learned to value myself, understanding that my well-being extends beyond my own existence; it impacts the lives of those who depend on me. To be a pillar of strength and support for my nieces, friends, and family, I must prioritize my own health and growth. Breaking the cycle of struggles that have affected my parents and ancestors is crucial; I refuse to pass on depression and bondage to future generations. By taking these steps, I hope to pave the way for a brighter, healthier, and happier future for myself and my unborn child.

When we persist in actions that cause us harm, the consequences are not always temporary. I reached a point where I realized I needed to break free from the cycle of self-inflicted pain and self-sabotage, which stemmed from the challenges I faced at home with my parents. My mother's illness took a toll on me, and I found myself reacting with a mix of pain and anger, as I was struggling with my own well-being. Ignoring the guidance of God led me away from living a life of integrity, which, in turn, resulted in difficult situations and outcomes.

Engaging in premarital sex at a young age had significant repercussions as I found myself unexpectedly pregnant at just eighteen. Aware of my lack of preparedness to responsibly raise a child, I made the difficult decision not to proceed with the pregnancy—a traumatic experience I had to confront and overcome.

In the past, I used to be slow to listen and quick to get angry, primarily because I was going through a lot of emotional pain and struggled to cope with the challenges I faced at home. This led me to lash out and engage in frequent fights. However, as I've grown, I have reached a point in my life where I have learned to love and value myself enough to prioritize peace above all else. It may sound cliché, but for me, peace translates to a life free from anxiety, heartache, and pain. I am committed to preserving this inner peace and won't let anything disrupt it.

God desires the absolute best for us, and to attain it, we must diligently pursue a meaningful relationship with Him. This has been my dedicated endeavor for several years, and truth be told, it remains a daily commitment because I value myself and yearn for God's finest blessings in my life. To achieve this, I have focused on building a deep and personal connection with the Divine. As a result, I have discovered a newfound love and appreciation for myself that I had never experienced before.

Devoting time to be with God has been pivotal in this journey. Regularly, I set aside moments for prayer, meditation, and reading His Word. In these moments of communion, I actively listen to God's voice, taking notes of His guidance and promptly acting upon it. Embracing this approach has helped me grow in faith and understanding, bringing me closer to God's purpose for my life.

My unwavering commitment to nurturing a relationship with Christ has yielded profound benefits, enabling me to love and appreciate myself in ways I couldn't have imagined. The journey of spiritual growth is ongoing, and I am eager to continue on this path of self-discovery and divine connection.

Building an intentional relationship with God can be transformative, propelling your life forward in a meaningful way. I have personally experienced the power of spending intentional time connected with God, creating a sacred space where distractions cannot interfere with our communion. In this space, I have been able to truly hear God's voice, and His guidance has been a constant companion, guiding me every step of the way.

Loving oneself is a journey that requires effort and dedication. It's not as simple as waking up one day and declaring, "I love me." Instead, it involves continuously challenging oneself and striving to improve in all aspects of life. For me, loving myself meant aligning my life with God's will, which required building a strong relationship with Him and putting in daily effort to nurture it.

Growing closer to God often means letting go of things that do not align with Christ's teachings. Initially, this process may feel lonely, especially if you have spent years without establishing a relationship with God and dedicating time to Him. However, I have found that even in the toughest times, God remains a constant source of comfort and strength. His presence is unwavering, even when people we love leave or disappoint us.

In essence, embracing a relationship with God has brought profound changes to my life. It has given me a sense of purpose and guidance, helping me navigate challenges and grow as an individual. The journey may not always be easy, but knowing that God is always there to support and love me unconditionally makes it all worthwhile.

Part of building a meaningful relationship is rooted in trust. Knowing that God has a plan for you, and everything will be okay, forms the foundation of this trust. I vividly recall numerous days and nights when I struggled with my singleness, feeling like my life was a complete train wreck. Though outsiders saw a facade of perfection and happiness, I knew deep down that I lacked both. During those trying times, I turned to cultivating my relationship with God. Opening my heart and speaking to Him in my brokenness, with tears streaming down my face, brought immense comfort. Realizing I could rely on God's love helped me navigate through the pain, gradually healing my wounds.

Yes, my single status brought moments of sadness, but I wholeheartedly trust that God has control over every fragment of my life. Remarkably, He has never failed me. Since establishing a connection with God and striving to align my life with His will, His presence has been unwavering. God consistently shows up for me, time and time again.

Discovering how to love oneself is a personal journey. As Christians, when we align ourselves with God, we also find alignment with one another. Consequently, we don't have to walk this faith journey alone; like-minded individuals will be sent our way. Finding purpose and filling the void within me became paramount. I yearned for a purpose-driven life that glorifies God. This pursuit continues relentlessly, and I'm committed to making shifts along the way. Embracing self-love necessitates reaching my purpose and living a life that resonates with it. God's love for us is boundless, and He desires that we live a life filled with purpose and meaning.

After years of healing, seeking forgiveness, and dedicating my life to God, I finally reached a place of wholeness. In that moment, God unveiled my purpose, and I embraced it with open arms. Standing in the midst of my purpose, I feel a profound sense of fulfillment. It brings me immense joy to know that God works through me to touch the lives of others, and when they look at me, they see His presence. Loving myself has become synonymous with fulfilling my purpose – helping others become better versions of themselves and aligning with God's will. True love lies in living with purpose, following God's guidance rather than our own desires. After all, if God cannot work through us to touch the lives of others, what impact do we truly have? Our existence serves a greater purpose, and we must lead the way for others.

Being truly committed to God and aligning yourself with His will requires continuous effort and dedication. It is not something you can simply do on Sundays and forget about the rest of the week. You need to actively work on strengthening your relationship with Him every day, and while it may be challenging, it is a beautiful and rewarding journey.

Loving yourself is a crucial part of this process. Embrace self-love in a way that exudes confidence, radiating from within you. How can you claim to love yourself if you lack confidence in the person you are? Remember that no one is perfect, and we all have unique paths to follow. Embrace your current place in life, stand firm in your beliefs, and have confidence in your journey.

One of my most significant qualities is my confidence and comfort in my own skin. Although I do have moments of self-doubt, I have always held a strong sense of self-assurance. My skin color, body, speech, and thoughts are all integral parts of who I am, and I take pride in them. Even when others choose a different path, I have the courage to follow my instincts.

Embracing confidence in yourself and your journey is essential. Trust in God's plan for you, be true to yourself, and find strength in your convictions. Remember that being confident doesn't mean being perfect, but rather embracing your imperfections and growing from them. Keep striving to be the best version of yourself and let your confidence guide you towards fulfilling God's purpose for your life.

I love myself enough to believe that with Christ's strength, I can achieve all things. There are no limits in the sky; I aspire to embrace everything God has called me to be and to find contentment in that identity. Regrettably, many of us underestimate ourselves and fail to explore the boundless possibilities life offers. In fifth grade, my teacher instilled in us the belief that success lies within our grasp, a truth that resonates profoundly with me. When we align ourselves with God's will, we unlock the potential to become anything we desire, fulfilling our divine calling.

In the past, I lived without purpose, disconnected from God's plan. Though others may have viewed me as successful, true growth and blossoming began when I surrendered to God's guidance. My ambition was to live a life brimming with purpose, refusing to limit God's work in my life. By doing so, I could play my part in bringing God's influence to this earthly realm and impacting the lives of others. Embracing God's path resulted in immediate success, accompanied by a constant stream of opportunities. It was a profoundly transformative and simple experience.

I refuse to settle for mediocrity or simply accept what the world considers good. My drive is to continually improve and surpass myself every day. This principle governs my life. I firmly believe that limiting ourselves to just one pursuit is selling ourselves short. We can have a fulfilling career, make a positive impact on the world and people, and run a successful business simultaneously. We are meant for more than just one thing, and it's crucial to love ourselves enough to embrace this truth.

Throughout the years, I meticulously penned down my personal goals. However, it wasn't until I learned to love myself that I realized the importance of aligning my goals with God's plan for me. I came to this realization through my own experiences, trying to do things my way, only to find disappointment. It became clear that living life for God was the only way that truly worked. I yearned for everything in my life to harmonize with His divine purpose for me. Often, we envision our own futures without considering whether they align with God's intentions for us. My greatest fear as an adult is finding myself in a place where God hasn't called me to be. Therefore, whenever I set goals for myself, whether they involve pursuing a promotion, embarking on a new career path, or relocating to another state, I engage with God from the very beginning. I earnestly pray about my decisions and listen for His guidance. With this approach, I never feel adrift. It's easier to stay on the right path rather than working hard to get back to where God intends for me to be if I deviate.

The beauty of it all is that God never abandons us. He constantly guides us. Embracing His way and doing things according to His plan brings an unmatched sense of fulfillment and purpose to life.

Staying focused is undoubtedly a challenging task that demands consistent effort and dedication every day. Personally, what helps me maintain focus is anchoring my mind on the promises that God has for me and the positive affirmations spoken over my life. However, I must admit that this journey towards focus often feels isolating. There are times when I must walk this path alone, minimizing distractions along the way. Loving myself has been a crucial factor in this process, pushing me to work on all aspects of my life and strive to achieve my goals without the option of failure.

Sometimes, we tend to view love as a one-sided emotion, but the truth is, it encompasses everything and is vast rather than limited. Learning to love oneself is not just a means to improve relationships; it is the foundation upon which we build a fulfilling life. By continuously working on self-improvement, we become the best version of ourselves and have more love to share with others. Conversely, when we are broken and lacking self-love, investing in relationships becomes a near-impossible task. Loving oneself is the key to being intentional in building healthy and meaningful connections with friends, family, and others.

Although we may face challenges and periods of solitude on this journey, it's essential to remember that God didn't intend for us to navigate life alone. Having a supportive community and walking alongside others can make the entire experience more manageable and rewarding. Staying focused and cultivating self-love are interconnected aspects that lead to a more fulfilling life with meaningful relationships.

Don't look back; keep going. You've come a long way, and God will never leave you or forsake you. Being a saved single woman, every day is not easy. A reminder that keeps me focused is going back to that gloomy day in the parking lot of my job when I asked God to come into my heart, forgive me for my sins, and poor decisions. And He did. Since that prayer, there has been no turning back for me. I took the leap, leaving Chicago and committing myself to change and becoming a better Candace. Moving forward without looking back was a decision I had to make, and I became intentional about giving my very best every day while trusting God. For me, that was an act of self-love, wanting to see myself at my very best. Giving up is not an option because I know I'll never get there if I do.

It's essential to remember that no one is perfect. God did not create us to be flawless, nor is that His expectation for us. Becoming better requires work, but I promise it will all be worth it if you allow God to cultivate you. My hope is that my story helps you connect with God and embrace the woman He has called you to be. Embrace the journey of becoming a better you!

Take care of your body, sis.
God gave you one body,
one mind,
one spirit,
one soul,
one temple.

God, I want to give you all of me. I am nothing without you, God. I know in order for me to have an honest and healthy relationship with you, I have to give you all of me. My heart, my mind, my soul, my body, I give it all to you. God, help me to heal and address everything that concerns me, and not ignore any hurt. Help me to challenge myself every day, so I can become a better me.

Amen.

Printed in the USA
CPSIA information can be obtained
at www.ICGtesting.com
JSHW021056171223
53850JS00001B/39